GOD AS AUTHOR

GOD AS AUTHOR

A BIBLICAL APPROACH TO NARRATIVE

Gene C. Fant Jr.

Nashville, Tennessee

Published by B & H Academic Publishing Group
Nashville, Tennessee

ISBN: 978–0–8054–4790–3

Dewey Decimal Classification: 225.6
Subject Heading: CHRISTIAN APOLOGETICS /
LITERARY CRITICISM

Printed in the United States of America
1 2 3 4 5 6 7 8 9 10 11 12 • 18 17 16 15 14 13 12 11 10
VP

For my grandparents,
who told me so many stories

In Piam Memoriam

Thomas Edison Fant (1909–1998)
Janie Irene Fant (1909–1991)
Joe Bailey Hankins (1908–1982)
Rosa Virginia Hankins (1904–1980)

Table of Contents

Acknowledgments   ix

Preface   xi

1 Making Sense of the Story   1

2 God as Author   35

3 What Does God's Story Look Like?   63

4 Finding God's Story in Narrative
      Structure   87

5 The Restoration Narrative in
      Literary Narrative   109

6 How Then Shall We Deal with
      Narrative?   129

7 Reading Redemptively   135

8 Writing Redemptively   159

Epilogue   181

Sources   185

About the Author   193

Name Index   195

Subject Index   197

Scripture Index   199

Acknowledgments

T his project is the fruit of a research leave funded by the Pew Summer Research Program at Union University, where I teach. That summer spent reading and wrestling with the concept of the lordship of Christ over my academic discipline of literary studies was, simply put, life-changing. I am grateful to Union's president, David S. Dockery, for his leadership in the cultivation of such thinking across our campus, even as I am grateful to our provost, Carla D. Sanderson, and the entire staff of our Center for Faculty Development for their support of such scholarship.

Portions of this project have been presented at professional conferences, including the 2008 Christ in the Academy conference held at the Stephen F. Olford Center in Germantown, Tennessee, and the 2006 and 2009 sessions of the Literature of the Bible subgroup, part of the annual meeting of the Evangelical Theological Society.

Other portions have been presented as a part of the worldview curriculum of Impact 360 (www.impact360.net), an annual program sponsored by the Lifeshape Foundation. I am grateful to the students in that program, who have helped me to flesh out my ideas, and especially to John Basie, for his mental and spiritual rigor. Mike Barnett also has been incredibly helpful in helping me to see that "Mission" is the fourth part of an effective Christian worldview.

Special thanks are due to an almost endless list of persons, but especially to my fellow dean Gregory A. Thornbury and to my dear colleagues Justin Barnard, Mark Dubis, Brad Green, George Guthrie, Hal Poe, Micah Watson, and to each of my colleagues in the Department of English, all of whom keep me on my toes and informed of others' ideas. Thanks is due as well to Rebecca Whitten Poe Hays, who helped me greatly in my research of materials, for students like she make me feel as though I should pay Union and not the reverse. To Suzanne Nadaskay, my administrative assistant, thanks for holding all those phone calls and taking all those messages.

For the folks at Broadman & Holman and Lifeway Christian Resources, especially Terry Wilder, thanks for the patience and assistance. I love editors!

Final thanks are due to my family, including my parents and in-laws. To my wife Lisa, apologies are due for the stacks of books and papers, and thanks must also be given for the endless conversations that trailed almost endlessly into the night on so many occasions. I am grateful for a wife who exceeds me in intellect at every turn. And to my kids, Emily and Ethan: Now I can finish that tree house. Whew!

In all things, glory be to God, whose story I can only repeat.

Preface

> Only be on your guard and diligently
> watch yourselves, so that you don't
> forget the things your eyes have
> seen and so that they don't slip
> from your mind as long as you live.
> Teach them to your children and your
> grandchildren.
>
> —Deuteronomy 4:9

I had an almost idyllic childhood, growing up on a narrow strip of farmland, which was squeezed between the foothills of the Alleghany Mountains and Lake Erie, in western New York. I was a transplanted Mississippian, my family having moved to the small college town of Fredonia to start new churches. Our parsonage, which doubled as a house church for several years, was on a little over seven acres, which bordered several hundred acres of grape vineyards, gravel pits, and, gurgling creeks.

The side yard had a tall and hardy hedge row that towered over my head. A narrow line of late-season daffodils grew along part of the hedges. When I played catch with a baseball or football in that side yard, the leaves of the bushes always felt cool as they brushed my cheeks whenever I reached past the daffodils to retrieve an errant throw.

One memory of that side yard stands apart, though. During probably the fall of my third grade, I was punting a football by myself, bored without anyone for a good game of catch. I would intentionally kick the ball straight up into the air and practice hauling it in against my chest. One punt went particularly high, and as I set my feet to catch it, something caught my eye. I can still hear the dull, almost metallic thud of the ball hitting the ground in front of me as I stood with my eyes fixed on the sky.

What I saw was the pale disk of the moon, ghostly white against the weak blue sky. It was almost the same grey-white as the few clouds that were visible. I suspect that the roundness of that full moon contrasted so starkly against the abstractions of the cloud shapes that it caught the corner of my eye.

"How is the moon visible?" I wondered to myself. "It's daytime. The sun is for the day; the moon is for the night".

I found my football and stretched out on my back, using the football as a pillow while I stared at the moon.

"How can I see it?" I repeated to myself. "There aren't any stars. Maybe after dark, I'll be able to see the sun!"

I waited until bedtime and sneaked out into the side yard. The full moon was still visible, but it had moved to another place in the sky. The sun, of course, was nowhere to be seen. I decided that perhaps the moon was sometimes visible during the day, as sort of a companion to the earth.

Some thirty-five years later, my own son was eight and in the third grade. One day Ethan asked, "Dad, why is it that I can see the moon during the daytime?" In that moment, all of my memories of that late fall afternoon came flooding back.

One of the joys of parenthood is the opportunity to ask questions posed by children. As a father, I never cease to be amazed at the complexity of the questions that my children offer up, even as I am vexed by the challenge of the simplicity required in my answers. Parenthood forces us to rethink many issues, from theology to science to storytelling. There is something powerful in this process, as our own understanding of these issues gains fresh insight from having to revisit our presuppositions about so many topics.

As an adult, I have burrowed deeply into a great range of subjects, and it is easy to end up knowing the minutiae but forgetting and then missing the beauty of so much of this world. Now I know the celestial mechanics that cause the moon to track in the sky in certain ways, but I rarely ever look up into the daytime sky and see the pale phantom of a moon that is visible during some days of the month. When Ethan, though, asked me why we can see the moon during the day when the moon is what shines at night, it forced me to translate my remedial understanding of the complexities of celestial mechanics, optical gradients, and reflectivity into language that may be understood by a young child.

More than this, though, is the secondary experience that I had when one of my children actually posed this question. In that moment, when I intentionally looked up into the pale blue sky for the first time in decades and saw that pale disk that seemed so far away, I was carried back to my own childhood. Further, I looked back in the sky to see the moon and was struck by a further realization: the pale contrasts of the moon, the clouds, and the sky were *beautiful*. It was not just a scientific epiphany; it was an aesthetic experience.

This is, in fact, the blessing and the curse of adulthood: we know the details and many of the answers, but we forget about the aesthetic component that possesses the power to move us so powerfully. As William Wordsworth once wrote, "Little we see in Nature that is ours; / We have given our hearts away, a sordid boon!"[1] The realities of life in the "real world" often strangle the mysteries of that very world out of our consideration.

Adulthood tends to treat experiences in dualistic and mutually exclusive terms: either they are rational or they are aesthetic. Poets have been fighting this false dichotomy for years, including John Keats's declaration at the end of "Ode on a Grecian Urn"

---

[1] W. Wordsworth, "Sonnet XXXIII: The World Is Too Much with Us" (1807), in *The Works of William Wordsworth* (Hertfordshire: Wordsworth Editions / Cumberland House, 1994), lines 3–4.

(1820): "Beauty is truth, truth beauty, —that is all / Ye know on earth, and all ye need to know" (lines 49–50).[2] Truth and beauty are so interlinked as to make them inseparable. If one mars truth, one mars beauty; the reverse holds true as well. Likewise, failing to consider beauty means that one has diminished truth.

Our intellectual age is one of schism. Many people have segmented the realm of truth to the world of science, even as they have relegated beauty to the world of aesthetics. Such a dichotomy is false and unfortunate.

As a literary critic, I engage in the application of rational analysis to aesthetic works. I walk the intersection of truth and beauty on a daily basis. The risk I run is that I could become so rational in the way that I treat a text that I oppress the beauty out of it. Anyone who has seen the classic film *Dead Poets' Society*, starring Robin Williams, will remember the scene where the textbook instructs the students to graph the work into a chart, wherein classic works may be compared to one another "objectively." In college, I myself was assigned the real textbook behind the incident, Laurence Perrine's bestselling *Sound and Sense: An Introduction to Poetry*. Such objectification of literary work misses the point of the magic that we call narrative, whether it is found in poetry or in prose.

Narrative is part of the glue that binds us together as humans. No matter the culture or the era, stories are ubiquitous. Wherever people gather with old friends, they tell stories about the good old days. At family reunions, we pass down the tales of our ancestors. As a nation, we share certain common narratives that help give us a sense of cohesion.

Ironically, even as narrative is a communal experience, it is also deeply personal. Small children tell rambling stories about their day's adventures. Elderly persons tell detailed stories about their experiences as small children.

Further, stories communicate truth in ways that are unparalleled, in part because stories are "sticky": we remember them in ways that we do not retain other forms of communication. This

---

[2] J. Keats, "Ode on a Grecian Urn," in *The Norton Anthology of English Literature*, 6th ed., ed. M. H. Abrams (New York: W. W. Norton, 1996), 1793–1795.

quality explains why narratives have influenced human thought so directly for millennia. In our age, for example, we face new challenges that have arisen from our new abilities in the area of biotechnology. Building on the tradition of P. D. James, Aldous Huxley, and George Orwell, contemporary novelist Kazuo Ishiguro's *Never Let Me Go* examines the issue of human cloning in a way that is both powerful and persistent in its truth telling. Such works present insight in personal, transcendent ways by combining the rational with the aesthetic, transcending mere abstract cognition. Cold, impersonal rationality is sometimes a hobbled skill, especially in issues of morality and conscience.

The fact that stories are *persistent* is indisputable. The *reason*, however, for this persistence is not readily understood. The fact that stories are *powerful* is indisputable; the *reason*, however, for this power is not clearly identified.

Humans have a propensity to take things for granted. We ignore details, even significant ones, presuming upon them even as we fail to notice them. Narrative is a little like that; for us it just *is*. We use it like water, failing to think about where it came from and how it really works. How it works and why it is there simply are taken for granted. We do not even think about it, even though it permeates our own lives as the pale disk of the moon hanging in the sky on a cool autumn afternoon also does.

Most of us have read that Christ is "the Author and Finisher of our faith" (Heb 12:2 KJV), so it makes sense that the gospel would be God's story. As many a church message board has noted so succinctly, "History is His story." In our easy discussions of special revelation, I cannot help but wonder if we have missed something awe-inspiring that may be revealed by a reversal of the lens that we turn toward narrative. Perhaps the gospel is not just like a story; perhaps story, narrative in general, is like the gospel. My clear conviction is that something stands behind the power of narrative. In fact, I believe that Someone stands behind it. There is an Author whose skill and grace imbue the broad range of the stories that we tell. There is a Father who gave us a story to help us understand our place in this world, a story that points back to Him.

His story is, in many ways, the only story that we know. When we use that realization as a foundation for interpreting and generating narrative, it changes everything, including ourselves.

A final word: As I was writing this book, I reread Charles Colson and Nancy Pearcey's *How Now Shall We Live?* and realized that they introduce each section with an illustrative story about the material that follows. I smiled in the realization that they employ narrative to facilitate understanding of their systematic approach to worldview. I hope that my readers will indulge me in some narrative digressions along the path I take. After all, what would a book about narrative be if it did not include a few stories? I appreciate the reader's indulgence as we look for God's story in *our* stories.

1

Making Sense
of the Story

When Philip ran up to it he heard
him reading the prophet Isaiah, and
said, "Do you understand what you're
reading?" "How can I," he said,
"unless someone guides me?" So he
invited Philip to come up and sit
with him.

—Acts 8:30-31

Persons attempting to find a
motive in this narrative will be
prosecuted; persons attempting to
find a moral in it will be banished;
persons attempting to find a plot in
it will be shot.

—Mark Twain (Samuel L. Clemens),
Introductory Notice to
The Adventures of Huckleberry Finn
(1884)

As a college literature professor, I introduce students to the concept of hermeneutics, the art (always) and science (sometimes) of interpretation. In my freshmen and sophomore classes, only a few students plan to continue in the study of literature, so I have my work cut out in terms of convincing them that this is actually a worthwhile venture.

Many of these students bristle when I try to teach them how to read critically. "Just give us the facts and let us memorize them," they seem to whisper when my back is turned. My plan, though, is that they will learn how to approach a story and analyze it, not only figuring out the basic trivia that may be gleaned from the story, but also looking to the insights that may be found and, ideally, applied to their own lives.

In my office I keep an object that I sometimes bring to class at the start of the semester. I pass it around, allowing the students to handle it and turn it in different directions. Quickly, they begin making guesses about its identity. From one angle, it looks like a small, funky paper weight; from another, a poorly shaped house. Over the years I have had all kinds of guesses, some reasonable and some comical. Interestingly, with very few exceptions, my students believe from their first glance that the object is made and not natural.

Little by little, I reveal information about it. I tell them that I found it in Florida. Some add guesses that it is an Amerindian artifact. I tell them that I found it on the beach. New guesses move into tools or specific uses for the object. I tell them that I studied Aztec culture extensively when I was in college. Then I turn the object to a specific angle and show them that from that angle it looks like a jaguar's head, with an open mouth and a perfectly rounded eye. At this point, they usually gasp and say something like "It's an Aztec Jaguar idol that washed up in Florida!"

My activity, though, is a trick. When I bring them the object, they have no context for interpreting it, for making sense out of it. They do not know if it is something artificially crafted or something that naturally occurred. Their guesses reveal their preconceptions of what such an object might be. In fact, they begin to mold their interpretation to fit these preconceptions even though they have very little actual information about the actual identity of the object. They place their ways of knowing what the object is over and against what it *really* is. As I add information, their guesses hone in on more specific preconceptions. I have done this for many years, so I have my technique down pretty well. It is fairly easy to manipulate their guesses.

The reality, though, is that while I did find the object on the beach in Florida, and while I did study Aztec culture in college, the two facts are not related. The object has nothing to do with the Aztecs; in fact, it is not an artifact at all because it is not man-made. I found it on a stretch of beach that has a kind of grass that grows through the soft compressed sandstone (I think it is sandstone anyway) that is just under the beach. When I found it, I saw piles of the stuff lying around, with these nifty, almost perfectly round holes where the grass had grown. This one piece had caught my eye, perhaps because *I* had studied Aztec culture, and its shape reminded *me* of a Jaguar idol.

In that original context, however, I did not interpret it as an actual idol. I just thought it was nifty, so I picked it up. When I took it back to my office, I realized how neatly it could help me illustrate the concept of hermeneutics.

For Christians, this activity is remarkably similar to how we view the world. On our own, left to our own devices, we grasp after half-thoughts and predispositions, trying to make sense of our world. Sometimes we strike interpretive gold and stumble across truth; sometimes we find ourselves convinced of our own interpretations only to find out, as additional information is revealed, that we have missed important clues or, worse, have been completely wrong.

Devotees of religious pluralism often use the analogy of the blind men who feel an elephant as a way to understand how humans view God. Kevin DeYoung and Ted Kluck outlined the analogy in this way: a group of blind men tried to figure out the identity of an elephant using only senses of touch; a trunk in one's hand, a tail in another's, and an ear in a third man's hand.[1] In turn, they declared their guesses based on incomplete information. Together, they began to piece together their guesses, attempting to puzzle together what was, to those who had sight of the process, a ridiculous guess.

DeYoung and Kluck's point was that this kind of blind religious pluralism displays a false humility in an effort to avoid appearing intolerant of or arrogant toward others' views. As they further pointed out, "What if the elephant spoke and said, 'Quit calling me crocodile, or peacock, or paradox. I'm an elephant, for crying out loud!' . . . And what if the elephant gave us ears to hear his voice and a mind to understand his message (cf. 1 Cor 2:14–15)? Would our professed ignorance about the elephant and our unwillingness to make any confident assertions about his nature mean we were especially humble, or just deaf?"[2] Or, I might add, downright rebellious? God reveals Himself in many ways, including through the Scriptures in particular, wherein He declares, "The whole of My being is much greater than what you are feeling with your blind hands!"

Texts are not elephants, of course, but to some extent, readers are blind men grasping after clues for what they are reading. In some ways, because texts are by nature challenging, it is a wonder that authors and audiences ever connect at all. Literary narratives include the challenges of language (writers and audiences must speak and share the same language), literacy (they must share at least basic literacy in that language), connotation (they must share an understanding of the words of the narrative, which shift over time and culture), the authors' generative skills (how they transfer thoughts into writing), and the audience's ability to interpret the text (how they process the text into their own understandings, both communally and individually).[3] The very nature of these

---

[1] K. DeYoung and T. Kluck, *Why We're Not Emergent (By Two Guys Who Should Be)* (Chicago: Moody, 2008), 37.

[2] DeYoung and Kluck, *Why We're Not Emergent,* 37.

[3] For a very helpful explication of the nonrandomness of language, especially written language, see B. Wicker and J. Witt's *A Meaningful World: How the Arts and Sciences Reveal the Genius of Nature* (Downers Grove: IVP Academic,

challenges means that texts cannot be random if they are to be sensible; they must be intentional, both in their generation and in their interpretation.

Contemporary literary criticism tends to exploit the fault lines between these challenges, shifting from the New Critic's hermeneutics of skepticism about the author to the currently voguish postmodernist's hermeneutics of outright antagonism toward the author and the text. Increasingly, the emphasis falls on the reader, which tends to convert literary works more into mirrors that reflect and indulge a reader's narcissism than into narratives that inspire and edify. In this kind of configuration, critics spend their time looking for randomness as they ignore the very patterns and structures that enable the search for the randomness that they pursue.

Writing classes, however, tend to seek a carefully balanced connection between the writer and readers. In expository writing, this emphasis is carefully pursued, with virtually every textbook containing a chapter on "audience," which discusses the importance of knowing the intended audience and shaping the message of the text to that specific audience. One of the most popular freshman composition texts in the United States, *The St. Martin's Guide to Writing*, for example, measures a text's success by "how well it achieves its purpose with its readers."[4]

Creative writing classes sometimes place emphasis more on the text itself as an art form apart from considerations of audience (*Be true to yourself through the text* is something of a mantra

---

2006), 30–57. Of particular interest is their discussion of the irrationality of the old canard about a room full of monkeys typing on keyboards for millennia and eventually producing the text of Shakespeare's *Hamlet*. The text of *Hamlet* is not a random set of written characters that are equivalent to any other set of written characters of the same length and complexity. Meaning is not constructed, or revealed, one letter at a time. The letters themselves are characters that reflect a particular stage of a particular language (Elizabethan English), a historical context (including the spelling and orthography of the words), a philosophical point of view, a dramatic structure, and many other factors. A text like *Hamlet* is not the production of a random set of letters in a specific order and sequence, but the production of a unique narrative that reflects uniquely human insights in unique ways.
[4] R. B. Axelrod and C. R. Cooper, *The St. Martin's Guide to Writing,* 6th ed. (Boston: Bedford / St. Martin's, 2001), 5.

for creative writers), but the audience issue is still important. In fact, the most common approach to teaching creative writing is called the "workshop," where students take turns providing their classmates with copies of their work, and the rest of the class then critiques the text, making suggestions for improvement and refinement. These workshops are pretty much focus groups of intelligent readers who provide feedback on whether or not the story makes sense outside of the author's own mind. The editorial process in publishing likewise underscores this connection between author and audience.

Chief among the critiques made in workshops is the issue not only of whether or not the story makes sense, but also whether or not it rises to the level of securing the reader's sustained interest. In my classes, I call this the "So, what's the point?" test. In workshop papers, the worst reaction a writer can produce is that where readers say, "That was lovely, but so what?" If the story lacks a point that captures the reader's interest, then the reader feels as though the time spent reading was wasted. Many writers, especially beginning writers, have a difficult time getting their ideas into a form where they communicate the point that they wish to make.[5]

The idea that narrative has meaning has been a bristling point for writers for several generations now. Even super-cynical Mark Twain shot a warning across the interpretive bows of the readers of *The Adventures of Huckleberry Finn*: "Persons attempting to find a motive in this narrative will be prosecuted; persons attempting to find a moral in it will be banished; persons attempting to find a plot in it will be shot."[6] Twain's irony aside, readers always have an impulse to determine the meaning of each and every narrative they encounter. Ultimately, hermeneutics asks this very basic question: "What's the point of the story?" Simple stories, like

---

[5] Many literary critics would say that these frustrations are evidence that texts never have authorial intent or even real understanding. I am dubious of such claims (as I will make clear in several places hereafter); I believe that much of our difficulty in language results from the so-called "noetic effects of sin" (the notion that through the fall, sin has harmed human intellect's ability to understand God, which I believe impacts our other rational pursuits).

[6] M. Twain (S. L. Clemens), *Adventures of Huckleberry Finn* (centennial facsimile ed.; New York: Harper & Row, 1987), 5.

fables, may have only one point (often called the "moral of the story"), while more complicated stories, like novels, may have a number of complicated points that surface on a variety of levels. All stories, however, communicate *something*; while experts may not agree on the *locus* of that meaning, a number of strategies have been developed to help understand stories.

What Narrative Is

Narrative finds its roots in storytelling. It can be oral (the earliest form of tale-telling) or literary (written stories, which I will emphasize in this work). Literary narrative should not be, however, limited to prose formats like novels and short stories. For my purposes here, I use "narrative" to describe any medium's ability to communicate a story. I follow other literary critics' practice of employing a very broad definition of the term that includes some poems and most drama.[7]

Most people think of narrative as fictional, which is certainly the most dominant form of storytelling, but it can also be poetic (even a brief sonnet or limerick can tell a story) or historical (the best histories are those that tell stories).

A cross-cultural, diachronic survey of the panorama of human narrative reveals a sweeping range of experiences that are both culturally significant for their original tellers but are also incredibly applicable to times and societies far removed from the source. When these narratives are written down as literature, they enter into a more stable mode of communication, for literary narrative has more permanence than oral forms and is infinitely more likely to be translated than are preliterate forms.

I define literary narrative as "the written expression of shared human experiences." The fact that it is *written* indicates a different form of conception, as there are clear differences between the way that we communicate to one another in oral and written contexts.

---

[7] See, for example, J. S. Brown and S. D. Yarbrough, *A Practical Introduction to Literary Study* (Upper Saddle River, NJ: Pearson Prentice Hall, 2005), 50: "We must be careful not to be too restrictive in our definition of narrative; it doesn't necessarily mean a story told in prose form. A dramatic work will almost always present a narrative, and many poems are narratives."

Anyone who has ever tried to read a good essay as a speech knows that it can be a challenge to shape words in new ways (since speech includes so many elements of paralanguage, which impact how the words are perceived). The reverse is true as well, as sometimes moving speeches fall flat on the written page.

Further, narrative is a uniquely *human* venture. Some years ago, comedian Steve Martin published a collection of short stories called *Cruel Shoes*. It is a quirky book, not a typical collection at all, but rather one that explores how imagination can be pushed and prodded in bizarre and sometimes disturbing ways. One of my favorite stories is "Serious Dogs," which was about an intellectually precocious pack of dogs given to melancholy daydreaming and snobbish pursuits like sharing expensive wine and Monet paintings.[8] The first time I read the story, I thought immediately of the Disney movie *101 Dalmatians*, which included the scene where the dogs all barked around the countryside, communicating to one another that the infamous puppies were missing. These notions of underground social networks of animal communication are just a couple of examples of how commonly our culture thinks about animals having vibrant modes of communication.

Animals do, of course, communicate with one another. We know that they send information to one another about food locations, danger, and other basic life situations. They do not, however, tell stories to one another, reliving hunts or adventures or romances. From what we can tell, animals are creatures of the moment, not the past. Moreover, animals do not write down those stories and preserve them for later generations.

Almost compulsively, humans tell their stories, repeating the details of the past, shaping them for effect, sometimes lying, sometimes creating tales out of new cloth. When we sit around campfires, we spin yarns. At the dinner table, we talk about our day. At family reunions, we pass legends along to the next generations. We read novels, essays, short stories, and epic poems that all unite us into cultures across time and nationality.

---

[8] S. Martin, "Serious Dogs," in *Cruel Shoes* (New York: G. P. Putnam's Sons, 1979), 31–36.

Narrative is as much a human distinctive as bipedalism or opposable thumbs. It partially defines us as a species. It is part of our material culture, binding us together across time and culture.

In literate societies, narrative spurs the production of literature. Literature is perhaps the most distinctively human of all art forms, far removed from any sort of vague emulation by a member of the animal kingdom. It is, in many ways, a transcendent mode of artifice precisely because of the way that it connects humankind. As James Sire noted, "Shakespeare—the writer who most fully displays the character of humanity—will always be able to be understood and appreciated, as will be Aeschylus and Homer, Cervantes and Goethe, Dante and Tolkien, Dickinson and Woolf. We grasp the humanity of those who left their marks on the caves of Lascaux thousands of years ago. There is a human nature."[9] Like the cave paintings, stories provide a means of connecting with other persons. Whether the stories become part of the *belles lettres* tradition or they are old folktales recorded into written forms by a researcher, narratives are consciously shaped to communicate with other persons.

Finally, narrative is about human *experience*. As a cornerstone of culture, narrative teaches our children about heroes and history, about God and goodness, about virtue and values. It shapes the future and teaches from the past. Narrative helps us to navigate the troubles that come from life, whether love, hate, fear, illness, or death. It helps us to share in the joys, hopes, and desires of this world as well. While language is bound up in culture, the basics of human experience transcend culture. We all experience love, regardless of how we might express that emotion. We all fear death in some way, regardless of how we might mourn that loss. We all rejoice at different times, regardless of where we might find or exhibit that delight.

Ironically, narrative employs universal experiences that define us as societies large and small. The body of tales that are common to our experiences are a part of what make us "American" or

---

[9] J. W. Sire, *Naming the Elephant: Worldview as a Concept* (Downers Grove: IVP, 2004), 156.

"Southern" or "postmodern" or "NexGen" or whatever. The stories that we tell become the shorthand that we use for witticisms or insights. If we want to impress one of our friends, we perhaps make an allusion to an inside joke that indicates that we have at least a few shared experiences ("he went on and on with that story, yada yada yada, and then I had to run screaming out of the room") or share the same interests ("happier than a man in a houndstooth hat at the Sugar Bowl"). When we gather together with old friends, we retell the same adventures, gaffes, and experiences ("and then he fell out of the boat and somehow got vertically half wet"). In the largest of all senses, narrative is a means of connecting our humanity with others. Narrative is a way to communicate truth to one another.

What Narrative Is Not

Narrative is not axiomatically "false," even as it is not always "true." It is, more times than not, imaginative, which means that it is arranged in a way to appeal to the imagination, to bypass the purely rational part of our minds, and to appeal to something deeper. Sometimes the base "facts" of the story are accurate in a kind of objective way, and sometimes they are invented or exaggerated for effect.

In our culture, we are used to nonfiction being the primary mode of communicating ideas. We read essays in print media, postings on blogs, and books about a variety of subjects that proclaim any range of thoughts. For the average person on the street, the difference between "nonfiction" and "fiction" is that nonfiction is true and fiction is, by definition, false. This simple duality, though, is completely wrongheaded. First off, a visit to the nonfiction section of any bookstore would be filled with confusion if everything on those shelves were to be considered as "truth." Further, a trip to the fiction shelves would not leave us lacking the great truths of the ages or, indeed, the faith. To dismiss a novel as a trifle, as insignificant simply because it is "fiction," is to completely underestimate the power of narrative.

One illustration of the power of narrative fiction comes from the nineteenth century: Harriet Beecher Stowe's classic novel *Uncle Tom's Cabin*.[10] The abolitionist movement in the United States of America changed many people's minds and hearts through the use of first-person testimonies by powerful speakers like Sojourner Truth and Frederick Douglass, as well as many newspapers devoted to the issue. The dagger that set the deepest mark, perhaps, was the fictional story of the horrendous Simon Legree and the other characters who populate Stowe's novel. While the story was an imaginative amalgam of many people's real life experiences, stewed together in ways that are both imaginative and emotionally effective, it was incredibly accurate in its overall depictions. The result was two-pronged: (1) the novel became arguably the best-selling literary work in America of the entire century, and (2) the novel's message pierced the nation's conscience in a way that fueled the antislavery mindset of many citizens. The powerful truths that undergird the novel communicated in particularly effective ways, precisely because it was a vibrant work of fiction rather than a dry essay on the evils of chattel slavery and man's inhumanity to his fellow man.

Fiction is not "false"; fiction is imaginative. Fiction may, in fact, be true, as the line between what is fiction and what is nonfiction becomes mind-bogglingly blurry in the case of storytelling. That is why I prefer the terms "story" and "narrative" and not "fiction," unless I am speaking specifically about the larger genre as a part of a specific analysis.

A further danger may creep into our thinking when we label literary narratives as "just fiction." By diminishing its nature, we tend to diminish our active thinking in a way that also works to our disadvantage. When critics wrote about the historical and theological failings of, say Dan Brown's *The Da Vinci Code*, some defenders claimed, "It's just fiction. Fiction by definition is false, so just get over it." That approach to literature generates numerous

---

[10] H. B. Stowe, *Uncle Tom's Cabin* (1852; repr., New York: Barnes & Noble, 2003).

problems, the most significant of which is that of reading passively and ignoring the reader's responsibility to read discerningly.[11]

One final point is that narrative is not isolationist. I once heard a prominent fiction writer asked what books she might take with her to a desert island. Her response was funny: She indicated that she would like a typewriter and several reams of paper so that she could write the kinds of books she would like to read. There is, however, a kind of fault in that kind of thinking.

Narrative is, ironically, both self-centered and communal. In the best kinds of stories, the author tells a story of his or her own choosing, which often includes autobiographical elements. The audience reads the story, sharing in both the reading experience and in the examination of the events and themes of the stories relative to their own lives. In the end, the story often becomes deeply personal as the reader finds a connection with the story. On some level, successful narrative fulfills one of two wishes for the reader: either "tell me a story about someone unique who is just like me" or "tell me a story about someone who is so evil or absurd that I can feel better about myself."

Narrative is the antidote to the alienation most of us feel at some point, for it is ultimately a communal activity. Writers articulate feelings and thoughts that we ourselves have found impossible to express. Writers, then, find affirmation in their audience. All of us find hope that rises above our individual statuses. As a Christian, I draw great strength, encouragement, and humility from the breathtaking scope of the Christian intellectual tradition that includes many of the greatest thinkers of the past two millennia. As a reader, I am a part of that community. As a writer, I am a conduit of that community. As a believer, I know that the community of fellow Christians is part and parcel of the Church itself;

---

[11] Recent discussions of the theological merits of controversial novels often include offhanded comments by reviewers that the novels were "fiction" and therefore "false" and unworthy of discussion. This happened commonly with D. Brown's *The Da Vinci Code* (New York: Doubleday, 2003) and W. P. Young's *The Shack* (Los Angeles: Windblown Media, 2007). Such dismissals are, I think, unfortunate and uninformed; theological flaws are significant, whether communicated through fiction or nonfiction.

writers and readers are all members of that esteemed Body and should never succumb to the temptations that may arise to focus on ourselves, following after Paul's admonitions in Rom 12:1–8 ("many parts in one body") and 1 Cor 12:12 ("the body is one and has many parts").

Each month, I attend a meeting of the Joseph E. Martin Shakespeare Circle, a reading group in my town that has been in existence since the late nineteenth century. We alternate readings between a Shakespeare play and a more contemporary work. The discussions are fascinating. There is nothing quite like sitting around in a circle talking about characters and our understandings of the narrative's themes. Of particular interest are the expressions that are made about very personal experiences that somehow have connected with the readers, experiences that then are shared vicariously by each of us seated in the circle. When I sit among my fellow members, I am keenly aware that I have stepped into a streaming community that is not static; it is a dynamic tradition that has extended now for portions of three centuries. We pass along ideas that will one day be passed along even farther. Each meeting reminds me that narrative connects us in ways that are mysterious and deeply personal. In this connection, narrative finds one of its great purposes.

What's the Point of Narrative and How Do We Find It?

While I teach college English, my undergraduate degree was not in English but in anthropology, with a biology minor. I assumed that I would pursue a doctorate in that field and naively viewed my university's general education courses as a waste of my time and money. One of the courses that I particularly wanted to avoid was the sophomore literature course that most students took. In fact, I successfully figured out a way to bypass it completely through a standardized examination.

I had enjoyed literature in high school and had been fortunate to have wonderful teachers, but in my mind literature was completely irrelevant to my ultimate career goal. "What's the point?"

was my constant thought when I read literature. I did not mean what is the point of the story (like I said, I had great high school teachers who gave me the tools necessary for that), but rather what's the point of "having" to read all that literature anyway?

Somehow along the way I ended up being the guy whose job it is to try to answer that question for the students in my introductory literature courses. That is why each semester I begin with a discussion that seeks to provide a clear rationale for the value of literary study, especially in a Christian context, like the university where I teach.

Narrative is powerful when it is living, when it is learned *from*, not *about*. When we reduce literary narrative to a collection of great stories that are important because they are merely a part of our shared heritage, we have reduced it to the status of "past" events and have made it, in many ways, disconnected from the present. We have driven the deadly stake of "irrelevance" through its very heart.

When we propose, however, that we may still learn from narrative, that we may find golden truths in its ideas, then we have maintained the vitality that has long been the primary goal of literary study. Learning from stories requires us to read in a way that is active, that seeks to find connection between even the most ancient of authors and the challenges of our own circumstances.

I constantly emphasize these connections in my literature classes. In Sophocles' *Oedipus the King*, we discuss how we share Oedipus' basic question about the relationship between human free will and external determinism, whether by supernatural forces or even by genetic destiny. Aeneas' temptation to remain in Carthage with Queen Dido in *The Aeneid* forces us to face up to our own temptations to settle for what is easy at the expense of what is risky. Kazuo Ishiguro's *Never Let Me Go* confronts us with the humanity of supposedly disposable persons (clones, actually, who were created to be sacrificed for the healing of their donors), which forces us to confront our own feelings toward persons who differ from us.

Certainly, a list of such connections would fill many volumes; truths exist that transcend time and culture and that fill the pages of literary narrative. These truths which may be passed on to others keep literary study alive and, indeed, make such study necessary for the education of a thinking person.

Literary hermeneutics, or more properly literary criticism, serves as an interpretive strategy for readers. It provides the reader "keys" for unlocking the meaning of a text. A variety of schools of criticism have developed over the centuries, each with its particular approach to applying the philosophical underpinnings of the critics themselves. Some deal more seriously with the text; some, with the author; some, with the historical era; and some, with the reader. Indeed, each school of criticism has its own starting place for interpretation.

While the various schools of literary criticism help to unlock various interpretations of texts, they are poorly equipped to explain why narrative works the way that it does or why humans respond to narrative in such a unique way. They tend to ask what literature does rather than what literature is.

Such a question is often called the ontological question. Ontology is the study of being itself, examining the nature of things before moving to questions of how those things function. While we may interpret narrative without understanding its nature, exploring its nature can provide insight into meaning. For Christians, it is important to explore how theological conceptions of human knowledge might influence such a question. Is there a Christian or even a biblical understanding of the nature of narrative that could explain *why* it works the way that it does, as well as why humans seem to respond in such powerful and moving ways to it?

Christianity and Narrative

All religions employ narratives to communicate their beliefs. The aforementioned function of storytelling to create and perpetuate a sense of community makes it a primary vehicle for religious faith. Christianity is no exception to this, even as Christ Himself was in some ways the chief storyteller. His genre of choice was the parable, a brief, pithy narrative that communicates insight through real-life (or lifelike) anecdotes. Parables are particularly effective at communicating truth powerfully. His use of parables demonstrated the affective power of that particular communication medium. Christ employed the genre so commonly that Matt 13:34–35 describes Him as always teaching in parables: "Jesus told the crowds all these things in parables, and He would not speak anything to them without a parable, so that what was spoken through the prophet might be fulfilled: I will open My mouth in parables; I will declare things kept secret from the foundation of the world." In fact, Christ was building on an Old Testament tradition of parables, for they are employed in Judg 9:7–15 (Jotham's parable), 2 Sam 12 (Nathan's parable about David's sin), Jer 18:1–12 (the potter's parable), and several passages in Ezekiel (chaps. 15; 16; 17; and 24).

Narratives fill the pages of the Bible, from the dramatic opening scenes in Eden to the New Testament's historical descriptions of the early church. The words "Bible" and "story" go together like "peanut butter" and "jelly." Interestingly, the Bible also is forthright in its depiction of the difficulties in interpreting its stories. When Christ shared parables, the disciples themselves were flummoxed in their search for meanings to the stories. Right after the observation in Matthew 13 that Christ constantly employed parables, the disciples come to him asking for clarification: "Explain the parable of the weeds in the field to us" (v. 36).

In the same way, when Christ made a postresurrection appearance to some disciples on the road to Emmaus, he opened the Scriptures to them, interpreting them in the light of His position as Messiah: "Then beginning with Moses and all the Prophets, He interpreted for them the things concerning Himself in all the Scriptures" (Luke 24:27). This explanation prompts the disciples, who finally recognize the risen Lord, to declare, "Weren't our hearts ablaze within us while He was talking with us on the road and explaining the Scriptures to us?" (v. 32). Luke, therefore, asserts that Christ Himself held what might be termed the final authority in the proper interpretation of the Scriptures.

Christ-followers hold a kind of hermeneutical power, however, as Philip's experience with the Ethiopian eunuch illustrates in Acts 8:26–40. Riding in his chariot, the eunuch read aloud (as was the habit in the ancient world) from a scroll of Isaiah. Philip ran alongside the chariot and asked, "Do you understand what you're reading?" (v. 30). The eunuch shrugged in frustration, "How can I . . . unless someone guides me?" (v. 31). After he invited Philip into his chariot, Philip employed a Christocentric hermeneutic, telling "him the good news about Jesus, beginning from that Scripture." Philip's example is important, for it underscores the importance of interpreting Scripture through the use of other Scriptures, as well as the importance of using the Incarnation as the ultimate rubric for understanding the entire arc of the Scriptures.

Most of us can empathize with the eunuch's frustration, whether in understanding biblical texts or other narratives. Casual readers often want to take the path of ease in handling narrative, asking for a simple, basic answer to "What's the point?" Philip led the eunuch to a more challenging place, one that was vulnerable, for it required the eunuch to begin in a place of humility where he must ask for help, admitting that he did not have the answers that he craved.

Proverbs 1:1–6 makes an incredibly bold statement about the proper understanding of narrative, stating that the proverbs themselves are enlightening for the right interpretation of all kinds of information:

> The proverbs of Solomon son of David, king of Israel: For learning what wisdom and discipline are; for understanding insightful sayings; for receiving wise instruction [in] righteousness, justice, and integrity; for teaching shrewdness to the inexperienced, knowledge and discretion to a young man—a wise man will listen and increase his learning, and a discerning man will obtain guidance—for understanding a proverb or a parable, the words of the wise, and their riddles.

The Proverbs themselves, however, are not the locus of this power. Instead, they teach us how to improve our understanding through a proper relationship with God: "The fear of the LORD is the beginning of knowledge; fools despise wisdom and discipline" (Prov 1:7). In a Christian context, hermeneutics and humility are related inextricably.

I bring up these passages because of the close connection between biblical and literary hermeneutics.[12] Biblical exegetes have always taken their task seriously, seeking ways to interpret passages that are consistent and faithful to the meaning of Scripture as a whole. The church fathers and later theologians developed a number of hermeneutical strategies. In the West, these strategies formed the basis of much of the way that readers interpreted non-biblical narrative as well.

Christianity's Relationship with Literary Criticism

Historically, biblical hermeneutics and literary criticism have always shared a close, if not always amicable, relationship since both pursuits are at least basically focused on interpreting text. From Augustine to Dante to even T. S. Eliot, C. S. Lewis, and J. R. R. Tolkien in the past century, Christian thinkers have had substantial and lasting influences on even the most secular of literary critics.

In Western intellectual culture, however, the past half century has seen both challenges to the literary canon and a radical shift away from traditional religious thought. One of the unfortunate

---

[12] Two texts are essential to understanding evangelical approaches to hermeneutics: G. R. Osborne's *The Hermeneutical Spiral: A Comprehensive Introduction to Biblical Interpretation* (rev. ed.; Downers Grove: IVP Academic, 2006) and K. J. Vanhoozer's *Is There a Meaning in This Text?: The Bible, the Reader, and the Morality of Literary Knowledge* (Grand Rapids: Zondervan, 1998). Osborne's approach to a consistent and rigorous recovery and application of meaning is a powerhouse of aid to the reader, and many of his general principles can be applied to nonreligious texts. Vanhoozer interacts with literary critics like Derrida, Rorty, and Fish, whose works have been employed to undermine biblical hermeneutics in ways that allow the reverse to occur: using biblically thorough hermeneutical approaches to undermine contemporary literary critical approaches.

results of this shift has been a decline in the understanding of just how influential the biblical tradition is on literary studies. I have heard, for example, a literary critic who specialized in Milton studies boast that he had never read the biblical sources of *Paradise Lost*. He claimed that it allowed him to generate "fresh readings" of the masterpiece, but I have a feeling that he was instead just misunderstanding much of the work or missing out on a significant portion of its brilliance. Literary studies are not the only place where a lack of understanding of historical Christian faith creates problems of interpretation; the same holds true in music, where students no longer can understand the subtleties of Handel's *Messiah* or even in the world of art history, where students look at European cathedrals' stained glass with blank, ignorant stares that are excused in the name of tolerance.

This antipathy has been matched by an anti-intellectual impulse on the part of many in the Christian community, where higher education and its activities are viewed as either vain or dangerous. Narratives that are strongly imaginative are especially cautioned against, as are those that are produced by pagan or secular writers. As Darren J. N. Middleton has observed, "Christian readers tend to dismiss secular fiction as theologically scandalous, because it promotes ideas that violate the so-called permissible bounds of traditional Christian speculation."[13] Just as contemporary secularists often separate themselves from the Christian intellectual tradition, these critics of the broader culture tend to cut themselves off from the larger intellectual culture that provides context for much of the human experience.

For any number of reasons, there is a dearth of understanding in contemporary literary criticism about both the influence of biblical hermeneutics on literary criticism itself and about the more basic influence of biblical narrative on literary works. Prominent literary critic Camille Paglia has lamented the loss of biblical literacy among critics and, especially, young artists: "Knowledge of the Bible, one of the West's foundational texts, is dangerously

---

[13] D. J. N. Middleton, *Theology after Reading: Christian Imagination and the Power of Fiction* (Waco: Baylor University Press, 2008), 1–2.

waning among aspiring young artists and writers."[14] Paglia, of course, joined the chorus of other critics such as Harold Bloom, E. D. Hirsch, and Robert Pinsky who have understood that religion in general is an incredibly powerful force in artwork of all kinds. Even without a reverence for the truths of the Christian faith, there certainly exists a respect for the power of the Christian tradition, especially in the realm of narrative.

I often use the example of one relatively small section of Scripture, the narrative of David's kingship over Israel in 1 and 2 Samuel, to illustrate just how pervasive biblical influence is. Several years ago, former U. S. Poet Laureate Robert Pinsky, a powerful force in contemporary American letters through his leadership in the Favorite Poem Project, visited my town to give a series of lectures and readings. In preparation for this, I bought two of his books, including *The Life of David*. Pinsky surveys David's rise to power and his reign, through all of its complications and disappointments.[15]

I was struck by how each page I turned to brought to mind how frequently David or his shadow appears in an incredible variety of literary works. First, *Beowulf* contained clear references to 1 Samuel 16–17, especially the famous battle with Goliath. The *Beowulf* narrative followed many of the outlines of 1 Samuel, from the challenges of Unferth / Eliab to the use of no forged weapons to the use of the slain challenger's own sword to cut off his head as a trophy. Second, Shakespeare's *Macbeth* inverted 1 Samuel's description of David's rise to the kingship over Saul. Both David and Macbeth were told through supernatural means that they would be kings, but while David specifically avoided harming Saul, Macbeth began a bloody path to the kingship. David rose successfully to the throne, while Macbeth ended up dressed in "borrowed robes" (1.3.108–09) that "hang loose about him, like a giant's robe upon a dwarfish thief" (5.2.20–21, which

---

[14] C. Paglia, "Religion and the Arts in America," *Arion: A Journal of Humanities and the Classics* 15 (Spring / Summer 2007): 1. http://www.bu.edu/arion/Paglia. htm (accessed May 2, 2009).

[15] R. Pinsky, *The Life of David* (New York: Shocken, 2005).

may allude to the biblical Saul's size, for he stood taller than other men, 1 Sam 9:2). Third, Faulkner's *Absalom, Absalom!* took its title from 2 Sam 19:4, and its depictions of the Compson family's decline mirrored the story of David's slide toward death and the subsequent conflicts that broke out in his family.

These examples come from only one Old Testament narrative, portions of 1 and 2 Samuel. An exhaustive discussion of the entirety of these influences would fill many volumes of an encyclopedia. If, then, the biblical approach to narrative has been so influential, then there should be a seat at the critical table for critics who are steeped in the applications of this approach.

Probably the most lasting portion of a biblical model is that of allegory. Allegorical readings of the Old Testament predate even New Testament thought. Ezekiel 17:1–2 links allegory with parable: "The word of the LORD came to me: 'Son of man, set forth an allegory and tell the house of Israel a parable'" (NIV).[16] Paul was steeped in this method of reading the Hebrew Scriptures, as he himself alludes to in Gal 4:24, when he refers to the covenantal relationship between God and Abraham's two sons as *allēgoroumena* in the Greek, which may be taken as "symbolic" or "illustrative." The early church looked to the Old Testament as a foreshadowing of the New Testament, with certain events like Moses' leading of the Hebrews prefiguring Christ's redemptive mission or Daniel in the lions' den foreshadowing the resurrection.

The strictest allegorical approach is the fourfold allegorical approach, which includes the literal (the text strictly followed), the allegorical (the text interpreted as symbolic of Christ), the moral (the text as a moral exemplum), and the anagogical (the text as finding fulfillment in the Church eternal).[17] While originally employed in biblical interpretation, under the influence of Augustine and, much later, Dante, it began to be employed in the reading of extrabiblical narratives.

---

[16] HCSB and KJV use "riddle" for "allegory."
[17] See, for example, the early discussion of allegory in the section on biblical interpretation in the current *Catechism of the Catholic Church* (New York: Image / Doubleday, 1994), 39.

This tradition extends far into the canons of literary interpretation as well, especially where allegorical typology is concerned. In Shakespeare's *Measure for Measure*, for example, Isabella was a Christ-type who willingly sacrificed herself in order to save her brother Claudio's life. Beowulf likewise was a Christ-type because he rescued Hrothgar's kingdom from the ravages of an evil monster, Grendel. Even non-Western works can be viewed through this filter, with Prince Rāma of the *Rāmāyana* standing as a Christ-type in the way that he suffered terribly in order to teach his people the importance of following after the will of the divine. Aeneas' temptation at the hands of Dido in *The Aeneid* can be termed a foreshadowing of Christ's temptation at the hands of Satan in Matthew 4 and parallels; just as Christ followed the will of the Father, Aeneas followed the will of the gods, in his own "duty-bound" way.

Literary types can also stand in for other biblical characters. Sir Gawain was a type of the biblical Joseph as he faced his own version of Potiphar's wife, the mistress of the household of the Green Knight. As I have already mentioned, Macbeth inverted King David in that he was told that he would be king, but instead of waiting his turn as David had, he pressed forward to kill Duncan and seize the throne.

Of course, there is consistent resistance to these bibliocentric or Christocentric views of literature even in some Christian circles today, viewing them as a kind of eisegesis, which reads one's previously conceived views into the text at the expense of other factors.[18] At best, such a view is considered "quaint"; at worst, it is irrelevant to contemporary intellectual culture.

In some contemporary literary critical surveys, the only real mention of distinctively Christian approaches to interpretation is that of allegory as a historical relic. As the academy has grown more hostile toward the role of faith traditions, the influence of even allegory has been translated away from its base in the Chris-

---

[18] I have to chuckle at this complaint, however, because it is exactly the kind of prioritization of the reader that so dominates much of contemporary theory. The complaint, I suspect, is not really about the reader's preconceptions as much as it is about anything that is subject to religious thought.

tian tradition and has been secularized into other approaches that employ the technique of allegory to other critical stances, treating it as simply a kind of symbolic substitution that often will appear in other modes.

Resistance to allegorical readings is, I think, quite unfortunate and shortsighted since allegory is in many ways the motherground of almost every kind of symbolic interpretation, including most contemporary theories. An illustration of this allegorical interpretation is the nursery rhyme "Jack and Jill," which may be read as a biblical allegory of the fall: Jack and Jill are types of Adam and Eve.[19] When they went up the hill, they were reenacting original sin, with their pursuit of the pail of water representing their quest for divine status. They fell down, literally and spiritually, with Jack's crown representing the loss of his original lordship within paradise.

Secular allegories for "Jack and Jill" may include these:

* *Feminist reading*: Jack and Jill represent the oppression of women through stereotyping. Jack is a type of men and Jill is a type of women. Jack's actions caused harm to come to Jill, who tumbled after him, following in the wake of his own great, arrogant fall.
* *Marxist reading*: Jack and Jill represent the proletariat workers of the world. Their access to the basic needs of life, even water, are controlled by those who at the top of the hill (the wealthy, of course, who always live in godlike splendor at the top of the hill) rejected them and threw them back to the valley where the other proletariats live.
* *Freudian reading*: Jack and Jill's adventure symbolizes sexual relations. The pail of water is a vaginate object that expresses the real goal of their hill climbing. The hill structure itself represents the physiological arc of sex; their fall was due to the immediate shame they felt, which suppressed their natural desires after the fact.

---

[19] Interestingly, the town of Kilmersdon in the Somerset region of England claims to be the site of the original story, so there may be a literal level of the story as well.

   *   *Deconstructionist reading*: Jack and Jill's tale is a per-
       fect representation of how the text itself undermines our
       understanding of meaning. We strive toward the pail of
       water that represents meaning, even as we know that just
       like well water is not found on a hill top, meaning is never
       truly found despite our best efforts. The reader falls down
       from this aspiration, even as Jack and Jill fell down, dis-
       abused of their illusions of meaning.

All of these readings are, in fact, kinds of secular allegory. In fact, one might argue that most forms of literary interpretation are, at their root, symbolic or allegorical.

    Biblical allegory, then, is a kind of literary typology, in that much of the literature of the Western tradition consciously or unconsciously emulates or outright copies the stories and themes that are found in the biblical text. In other ways, the intellectual culture that has resulted from the Christian intellectual tradition has likewise shaped exactly how we look at almost everything, whether Western or non-Western. Like it or not, it is a seminal foundation of contemporary intellectual culture.

Christian Approaches to Narrative and Contemporary Literary Criticism

    When the editors of the first compact edition of *The Harper American Literature* anthology[20] moved into the second edition of the text, I went through the table of contents to update the page numbers of the literary works that I used in my Survey of American Literature course. When I got to Longfellow on my syllabus, I was shocked to find that the anthology had dropped him from their canon. Longfellow was one of the towering figures of our national consciousness in the nineteenth century. In fact, when I reviewed the introductory chapter to the "Literature of the American Renaissance 1836–1865," the literary period where his works had previously appeared, I noted that Longfellow was mentioned

---

[20] D. McQuade et al., eds., *The Harper American Literature*, compact ed. (Philadelphia: Harper and Row, 1987).

at least six times. The introductory chapter even includes a quotation from Nathaniel Hawthorne from 1855 that states, "No other poet has anything like your vogue."[21] The chapter goes on to note that Londoners snapped up 10,000 copies of his *The Courtship of Miles Standish* on its initial *day* of publication in 1858.[22] His influence was hard to ignore, even if the editors had determined that he was no longer worthy of inclusion in the reading selections because his literary reputation had "collapsed."[23] Longfellow's bust still resides in Westminster Abbey's famous Poets' Corner, alongside Chaucer, Spenser, and Shakespeare, although his poetry no longer appears in some mainstream anthologies.

Sometimes I have a similar feeling when I consider the place of Christian literary criticism. Basic handbooks of literary terms include numerous terms that derive from the days when biblical hermeneutics and literary criticism were close twins: "allegory," "anagogue," "epiphany," and so forth.[24] Further, some of the critics who have influenced contemporary literary criticism the most, such as Augustine, Dante, and T. S. Eliot, are cited in historical surveys, but these surveys rarely link the philosophical rationales explicitly to the critic's faith. Even more, the effects of these approaches to reading are dimly connected to their specifically theological understandings of text and authorship.

I mention these thoughts not to lament what some might term the sanitizing of the Christian intellectual tradition from the secular classroom, but rather to remind Christian readers of the great heritage that stands before us in examining how theology might bring us fresh breaths of understanding.[25] In fact, I think

---

[21] Quoted in D. McQuade et al., eds., *The Harper American Literature,* 2nd ed. (Philadelphia: Harper and Row, 1996), 526.

[22] Ibid., 526.

[23] Ibid., 422.

[24] One of the most prominent literary handbooks in current use is W. Harmon and H. Holman's *A Handbook to Literature,* 10th ed. (Upper Saddle River: Pearson Prentice Hall, 2006). This handbook includes a significant number of terms with Christian origins, but there is scant discussion of the influence of Christianity on literary criticism as a whole. The entry on "allegory" has almost completely sanitized the term's Christian roots.

[25] I do not, of course, discount the outright hostility that some Christians find in the secular academy. The level of discomfort that some secularists feel toward

that one of the great sins of our current intellectual culture is that of "chronological snobbery," to use the term coined by C. S. Lewis and Owen Barfield, the belief that what is old is irrelevant or quaint and not really useful for our work today.[26] Such an attitude forces us to reinvent the wheel, so to speak, even as it leads us to create self-congratulatory ideas that appear to be new but rather are just co-opting of older theories now forgotten.

The idea that narrative has inherent meaning, whether in the text itself or in the minds of the author or the reader, has a most refreshing sense, given the cynical state of literary studies. Indeed, the idea that such a meaning might evoke a kind of transcendence is even more radical.

A Hermeneutics of Optimism

Contemporary intellectual culture is dominated by worldviews that are both skeptical and cynical. While healthy doses of skepticism and cynicism are useful as tools when approaching various topics, when they become the dominant attitudes that one has toward life in general, the result is numbing. As many critics have noted, including Paul Ricouer, the hermeneutics of suspicion is the rule of the day in literary studies.[27]

Critics employ suspicion as their default mode to approach the text, the author, and even language itself. Not only is the notion of transcendence giggled at, but the notion of meaning itself has become so undercut that it is difficult to discuss in some literary circles. Implicit in these suspicions is a meaninglessness that translates not only to the relationship between persons but also to the universe itself. Perhaps American writer Stephen Crane best articulated this sense of brokenness and emptiness as far back as 1899, when he penned these lines: "A man said to the universe: /

persons of faith is matched only by the strength of some Christians' impulse to withdraw to a position that criticizes rather than engages the secular academy.

[26] C. S. Lewis, *Surprised by Joy: The Shape of My Early Life* (Boston: Houghton, Mifflin, Harcourt, 1995), 207–8.

[27] Ricouer identifies the trinity of Marx, Nietzsche, and Freud as the "masters" of the "school of suspicion." See *Freud and Philosophy: An Essay on Interpretation* (New Haven: Yale University Press, 1970).

"Sir, I exist!" / "However," replied the universe, / "The fact has not created in me / a sense of obligation."[28]

The effects of this suspicion and brokenness on the overall attitude of the humanities in particular have been significant. As critic John North has noted,

> The Humanities have lost their way in the last two decades. . . . Students seem to be arriving at the same conclusion, voting with their feet by walking away from the humanities so that across North America humanities student registrations drop markedly. Senior undergraduate and graduate students remark to me that they are moving away from English studies because the literature classroom is so heavily politicized, so technology-focused, and because postmodernism and critical theory are so dismissive of the text for its own sake on its own terms that they cannot study literature itself. In other words, our young people are sick of our sickness.[29]

Furthermore, the hermeneutics of suspicion does not comport with most people's experience of life. We long for meaning. We long for connectedness. We long for hope. We long for answers that bear some sort of transcendence for the challenges that face us in life. Terry Eagleton observed in his landmark work *After Theory*: "Cultural theory as we have it promises to grapple with some fundamental problems, but on the whole fails to deliver. It has been shamefaced about morality and metaphysics, embarrassed about love, biology, religion and revolution, largely silent about evil, reticent about death and suffering, dogmatic about essences,

---

[28] S. Crane, *The Red Badge of Courage and Selected Prose and Poetry,* 3rd ed., with an introduction by W. M.Gibson (New York: Holt, Rinehard and Winston, 1968), 640.

[29] J. North, "The Text's the Thing: Reflections from the Humanities," in *The Two Tasks of the Christian Scholar: Redeeming the Soul, Redeeming the Mind,* ed. W. L. Craig and P. M. Gould (Wheaton: Crossway, 2007), 166–67.

universals and foundations, and superficial about truth, objectivity and disinterestedness."[30] In many ways, theory has condemned itself to irrelevance because it has lost its relevance to the mainstream of most persons' lives and experiences. Critics themselves are feeling this frustration, including Mark Edmundson, who declared, "If I could make one wish for the members of my profession, college and university professors of literature, I would wish that for one year, two, three, or five, we would give up readings [of] Marx's, Freud's, Foucault's, Derrida's, or whoever's."[31]

Perhaps writers feel this loss of relevance more than do critics, who tend to live in fairly circumscribed worlds. Writers must engage with larger worlds, and this makes even the most cynical of writers something of an optimist: only the most masochistic or egocentric of writers would produce narrative that held no meaning or connectedness with other persons. One of my favorite writers, Eudora Welty, once termed the goal of good writing as one of good will: "Reader and writer, we wish each other well. Don't we want and don't we understand the same thing? A story of beauty and passion, some fresh approximation of human truth?"[32] For Christians, we might expand that approximation to include transcendent truth that is connected with God.

One of the ways that Christianity can contribute to literary criticism and hermeneutics is by emphasizing its specific distinctives: connectedness, hope, and purposeful meaning. I term this a hermeneutics of optimism. By this I mean that a cogent approach to narrative that is distinctively Christian will reflect these elements, each of which both demands a sense of optimism (that connectedness, hope, and purposeful meaning are possible) and produces a sense of optimism (that connectedness, hope, and purposeful meaning are identifiable in narrative).

---

[30] T. Eagleton, *After Theory* (New York: Basic Books, 2003), 101–2.
[31] M. Edmundson, "Against Readings," *The Chronicle of Higher Education*, April 24, 2009; posted at http://chronicle.com/weekly/v55/i33/33b00601.htm (accessed May 2, 2009).
[32] E. Welty, *On Writing*, with an introduction by R. Bausch (New York: Modern Library, 2002), 28.

The current secular emphasis on brokenness and difference has a stark effect on the handling of narrative. I am mindful of E. M. W. Tillyard's comment about the scholarly handling of the conflict between the Puritans and their opponents during the early seventeenth century: "[T]he Puritans and the courtiers were more united by a common theological bond than they were divided by ethical disagreements. They had in common a mass of basic assumptions about the world, which they never disputed and whose importance varied inversely with this very meagreness of controversy."[33] Tillyard's comment lamented how critics constantly dwell on the conflicts between the two camps, but almost completely ignore the reality that they were significantly unified in terms of their basic theology (their theism, their use of biblical text as authoritative, and so forth). In fact, the two groups shared the same basic worldview assumptions; the *applications* of those assumptions were where their differences lay.

Tillyard's lament over the scholarly focus on relatively minor difference in the midst of overwhelming similarity underscores the urge toward negativity that runs rampant in the critical community. Some of this may be justified since similarities often are *boring*. The lesson, though, is highly applicable to contemporary literary criticism. Our current obsessions with "the other" and, particularly, with *différence* in our own vocabulary (as Saussure called it) have a tendency to leave us in a quagmire of subjectivity. We have moved from asking "What does this text mean?" and arguing among the proposed answers to asking "Can the text mean anything?" and folding our arms across our chests, ready to dismiss *any* proposed answer.[34]

When I teach literary criticism, I always ask my students to analyze the logical fallacy of that final question. In order for the

---

[33] E. M. W. Tillyard, *The Elizabethan World Picture* (New York: Vintage, 1959), 4.

[34] We should not get bogged down into arguments about what is *the* meaning of the work or even the priorities of the meanings. I am not saying that those arguments are wrong, but I am saying that they are not the ultimate question. The ultimate question is *"Why* do stories have meaning?" Even if the postmoderns are correct, and I do not think that they are, and there is a multiplicity of meanings, each subjectively governed by the mind of the reader, the question still remains, "Why do stories have meaning?"

text *not* to mean anything, a printed question itself cannot mean anything. In order to ask the question itself, much less to consider its ramifications, we must perform an old-fashioned "willing suspension of disbelief" in the very terms of the question itself. The logical implications are, of course, staggering.

What I ask my students to consider is the hermeneutics of optimism, a way of looking at the text in a way that is critical but not cynical, probing but not suspicious, that is a way that seeks connection rather than isolation. This is why I stress the communal nature of narrative. The reader participates in the process not through the creation of subgroups (which end up spiraling into subjective / individualistic ramblings that are solipsistic or egomaniacal) that randomly assign meaning but by entering into an agreement with the writer that there *is* meaning in the text and that the author and the audience can connect with one another, creating a relationship of sorts that not only identifies meaning but carries it directly into the hearts, minds, and souls of the readers, applying it to their own lives in ways that are life-changing.

Writer Paul Thigpen believes that Christianity has an amazing offer to share with the world of narrative, a belief that with an injection of faith, approaches to narrative

> to one degree or another, explicitly or implicitly, will somehow reflect the vision at the heart of the gospel. It will operate on the assumption that despite our brokenness, despite the apparent futility of much that takes place in our world, life is ultimately meaningful, because we are not the result of chance, we are not alone, we are in fact loved; and because we are loved, we too can love. Christian literature will view the world in a way that reveals its sacramental reality. It will breathe an atmosphere with the scent of divine grace.[35]

---

[35] P. Thigpen, interviewed by D. J. N. Middleton, *Theology after Reading: Christian Imagination and the Power of Fiction* (Waco: Baylor University Press, 2008), 187.

As a writer, Thigpen believes that this is the central mission of the writer of faith, but his comments are relevant for the critic of narrative as well.

The avalanche of critical approaches that are hostile to faith have created a variety of responses from Christian scholars. This has been particularly true in the case of postmodernism, post-structuralism, and deconstructionism.[36] Such engagements have been helpful in evaluating these approaches, but there is a sense in which such engagements have seduced Christians into their own form of the hermeneutics of suspicion. The result has been to eschew such approaches altogether rather than to find ways to filter out the useful from the erroneous (or outright dangerous!) in such critical worldviews.[37]

Literary apologist Mark Bertrand has observed that "culture isn't shaped through criticism," and while he was discussing the importance of artists, rather than critics, shaping the larger culture, his words are applicable to the subculture of criticism as well.[38] When Christian literary scholars succumb to their own hermeneutic of suspicion and generate critiques of other schools of criticism to the exclusion of generating scholarship that reflects a theologically sound approach to narrative, then we have withdrawn from active shaping of the culture of criticism.

A hermeneutics of optimism views even contrarian approaches in ways that are gracious, even as it generates a humble, positive alternative. For more theoretically oriented approaches to narrative, I highly recommend Alan Jacobs' classic, if underappreciated,

---

[36] I often joke that there is little in these approaches that could not be cured through a year-long teaching assignment of freshman composition courses, where the more egregious flights of fancy that these theories sometimes entail are proved false on an almost daily basis. On a more serious note, however, I have a hard time believing that most critics of these schools would be very happy with other critics employing those very approaches to their criticism.

[37] J. K. A. Smith has a very helpful volume in the other direction, helping Christian critics to see cracks in the armor of postmodern theories, even as he sees usefulness in them: *Who's Afraid of Postmodernism: Taking Derrida, Lyotard, and Foucault to Church* (Grand Rapids: Baker, 2006).

[38] M. Bertrand, *(Re)Thinking Worldview: Learning to Think, Live, and Speak in This World* (Wheaton: Crossway, 2007), 187.

A Theology of Reading: The Hermeneutics of Love.[39] Jacobs up-
dated the Augustinian approach to narrative and added Bakhtinian elements that underscore what Jacobs called the "law of love."
By this, Jacobs meant that the Great Commandment ("love God"
and "love your neighbor") has weight as a guide for the interpretation of narrative. As readers, we are to hold a stance of love /
charity toward the author and, by extension, the text itself, which
is the bridge between the writer and the audience. His work has
greatly influenced many emerging scholars in the field of literary
studies.[40]

The weight of this optimism has begun to impact contemporary literary criticism. Notable critic Terry Eagleton has indicated
his embrace—however cautious—in *After Theory*. Even reader
response guru Stanley Fish has lately shown signs of employing
approaches that are surprisingly optimistic toward the text and authorial intent. All in all, there is a trend toward a new place at the
table for Christian approaches to literature. Thigpen believed that
this is because

> we cannot separate literature from theology any
> more than we can separate word from thought.
> Every work of literature breathes out a particu-
> lar theological vision of reality. Even an atheistic
> vision speaks about God by denying Him, and
> a secular vision speaks about God by ignoring
> Him. At the same time, every enduring theology
> ultimately finds a voice in literature. The Chris-
> tian gospel especially is at its heart a living story,
> not an abstract system. In the image of the God
> it proclaims, its thought must be expressed as a
> word that becomes flesh and dwells among us.[41]

---

[39] A. Jacobs, *A Theology of Reading: The Hermeneutics of Love* (Cambridge,
MA: Westview, 2001).

[40] A notable extension of Jacobs is S. Heulin's "Peregrination, Hermeneutics,
Hospitality: On the Way to a Theologically Informed General Hermeneutics,"
Literature and Theology 22 (2008): 223–236.

[41] P. Thigpen, interview by D. J. N. Middleton, *Theology after Reading*, 186.

Perhaps a shift is occurring that will breach the surreptitious wall of separation between criticism and theology. Like Thigpen, I cannot separate the ideas of theology and criticism because I cannot separate the ideas of Author and Story, as understood in the light of biblical text. If we understand God as an Author in the light of the biblical text, then there are going to be hermeneutical applications that must be brought to bear in our understanding of narrative as a whole.

Finally, a hermeneutic of optimism also restores narrative to a place of primacy in the world of text, and not simply in terms of the value of the text itself but rather in the sense of prioritizing narrative over criticism. In literary studies, the past two decades have seen the reverse occur with frequency, with the prioritization of criticism over (and sometimes even to the exclusion of) narrative itself. In such a shift, graduate students in particular find themselves reading less and less material relative to the criticism that they consume. I have heard many students who have dropped out of graduate programs identify this inversion as a chief reason for their change in goals. As one told me, "They criticized the love of literature right out of me."

The same occurs in biblical studies as well. A professional acquaintance told me of his experience in one of America's oldest and most influential divinity schools, where he had completed a program in biblical studies. As he packed up his apartment to move to his first pastorate, he placed his books into boxes and picked up his Bible. To his shock, he realized that he had not actually read it in two years. He had read it in Greek and Hebrew as a part of his explorations of higher criticism, demythologization, and other critical approaches, but he realized that he had not actually read it in terms of simply reading its narratives during this time. He determined to postpone moving into a pastoral role until he had reintroduced himself to his original passion for the Scriptures. This man's experience was hardly unique.

A hermeneutics of optimism would restore just this kind of passion for narrative, including biblical narrative. It reflects the shared community of fellow creatures, the hope of the gospel, and the purposefulness of meaning that God Himself has revealed to us, both of Himself and of the world as a whole.

I propose a further extension of these kinds of interpretive approaches: I believe that narrative meaning can find its grounding in the revelation of God Himself, and that hermeneutics can be viewed optimistically because its very nature reflects the ultimate hope of humankind: grace. In the interpretive frame that I propose, we find echoes of grace, it seems, almost everywhere we look in narrative traditions and in the world at-large. Because narrative is at its base oriented toward connectedness, it is best understood through the lens of God's self-revelation to His creation.

2

God as Author

Jesus stooped down and started
writing on the ground with His
finger.

—John 8:6b

_____

I was determined to say nothing
that I did not feel from the bottom
of my heart to be true and right.

—Booker T. Washington,
Up from Slavery (1901)

I have taught introductory literature courses for many years. It is my great joy to guide students through the various ways of looking at narrative to gain a stronger sense of understanding from the poems and stories.

Once when I was teaching William Faulkner's *A Rose for Emily*, a macabre little tale of an elderly spinster who died in an ancient house, I worked through the way that the text foreshadowed the unfolding of the events. I mentioned how the narrator assumes a voice for the entire community, a sort of chorus that echoes the kind employed by the Greek dramatists in their classic plays.

One of my students snorted, "I just don't see it. I don't see anything that you are talking about. The narrator says, 'We'; so it's more than one person talking. And they live in Mississippi, not Greece. And this whole thing you are talking about with foreshadowing, I think you are just reading your own ideas into what the words say. The words say what the words say. That's all they mean."

My student was invoking a literalistic principle, that words mean only one thing, as though when they are put together, they are completely independent units of meaning that have no connection with one another. "We" means "we" and can only mean the most basic definition of the term, "first person plural pronoun." It cannot reference anything but the very denotation of the word.

I explained that if she were going to insist on a very narrow definition of "we," then it meant that she herself had to join in the narration, as "we" includes "me." By not joining in herself, she was implicitly noting the connotation of the term, that there could be a distance between "I" and "we" that would allow "we" to include third persons who are speaking together as a unit. If that were possible, then the "we" could even include a set of literary traditions, like the Greek chorus, that would amplify our reading of the story, to see just how complex the narrative really was.

One of my challenges is that of teaching my students to learn how to read things literally when they are meant to be read literally and to read them in other ways, including symbolically or allusively, when they are meant to be read in those ways.[1]

As I have previously stated, literature is imaginative, which means that it is not *only* literal. It may be interpreted in a wide range of ways; this is why there are so many ways to treat texts through literary criticism. Literary narrative includes imagery, metaphors, allusions, and many other characteristics. Even genre itself (literary categories) impacts the way that we read.

The ability to operate beyond the literal distinguishes narrative from other kinds of communication. A manual on how to assemble a bookcase should be taken literally. Perhaps a cheeky student could argue that the manual tells the story of a person who is assembling a piece of furniture from pre-arranged pieces, and that symbolically the story is about how every person must learn to put his or her life together with the pieces of, say, education, relationships, and talents. Because it connects the writer and the audience, it maintains sort of an echoic effect from narrative's foundational characteristics, but the reality is that a manual is really just a manual.

Most persons have a default mode of literality in their speech and in their handling of narrative, even as they usually include a failure to understand how a literal sense of words undercuts and, indeed, makes the sense of these words humorous. For example, a colleague once told me of a student, a youth ministry major, who declared in class, "I want to be literally on fire for Jesus!" The student did not mean that he wanted to be a martyr for the faith, burned at the stake, but rather that he wanted his life to be white-hot in its passion for following Christ. What that student meant, of course, was that he wanted to be *metaphorically* "on fire for Jesus." The difference, of course, is critical.

---

[1] I am, of course, extending W. A. Criswell's famous statement about how to read the Bible in *Why I Preach that the Bible Is Literally True* (Nashville: Broadman Press, 1969), 90: "The whole Bible I preach literally, as being literally true. When the words are not to be taken literally but are representative and figurative, such a fact will be clearly indicated and it will be most obvious. The context will reveal it and the Scripture passages before and after will inevitably indicate it."

The Role of Metaphor in Narrative

One characteristic that imbues narrative (including narrative poetry) is that of metaphor. Metaphor is a comparison between two things that helps the audience to know more about the subject. When a poet says, "My beloved is a rose," the audience knows that what is meant is that knowledge about a common object, the rose, helps us to understand the qualities of an uncommon object, the poet's beloved. The poet is not saying that he is in love with a plant (well, except for in the medieval work *Roman de la Rose*), but rather that the prized qualities of a particular plant are ones that remind him of his lover's own qualities. The lover is not diminished by such a comparison; the audience, though, finds a greater understanding through the comparison.

Metaphors appear frequently in poetry, reaching a kind of peak in the Metaphysical poets of the English tradition, who employed elaborate similes (which are metaphors that employ direct terms of comparison, such as "like" or "as") in an effort to explore the expansive nature of love. Metaphors fill all sorts of narrative, however, from the simplest parables to the most complicated novels. The imagery that they provide, extending the power of the text to communicate ideas, is central to the overall effectiveness of story.

All human language is rooted to some extent in comparisons; some are explicit while others are implicit. Almost all adverbs in English are based on comparisons, for example. In Old English, most adverbs were formed by adding "like" (actually "-lic") to adjectives; after a few centuries, the "ke" ("c") dropped off the suffix, and the "i" changed to a "y," making "ly" the normative suffix for adverbs. So, "quick-like" became "quickly." "Hard-like" became "hardly." Some adjectives are formed in the same way: to be "God-like" is to be "godly." This is just one of the ways that comparisons form much of our vocabulary and imagery.

Metaphors typically have two parts, the tenor (the term that receives the comparison) and the vehicle (the term that provides the comparison). In the statement, "my beloved is a rose," "beloved" is the tenor that receives the attributes (softness, loveliness, etc.) of the vehicle, the "rose." Some critics replace "tenor" / "vehicle" with other terms, including "ground" / "figure" or "target" / "source." For our purposes, I will employ tenor / vehicle.

Metaphors are particularly useful in exploring abstractions (ideas) through concrete (physical) images. A classic example of this might be found in Machiavelli's *The Prince*, which portrays Fortune as a Woman. He then describes in great detail how the comparison works.[2] Even the naming of commercial products is often linked with metaphor. When Ford called its subcompact car the "Pinto," it was supposed to convey an exciting young colt that was full of oats, a sort of lesser version of the "Mustang." The same logic applies to the Dodge "Charger" (another horse metaphor, as opposed to the large, decorative plate that goes under a smaller plate in a formal table setting), the Pontiac "Firebird" (a sports car that invoked the mythical power of the dangerous, glowing bird), or the Nissan "Armada" (an oversized SUV, whose designers evidently were not aware of the date 1588 in English history).

Biblical Metaphors for God

In some theologically conservative circles, the employment of literary tools in biblical interpretation evokes a sense of anxiety. The fear is that a high view of the inspired status of Scripture as a unique and singular kind of text will be diminished through the use of what some might call secular tools in the deliberation over meanings of revealed Truth. While I understand such trepidation, in part because of my own high view of Scripture, fears of this sort should be remedied by a combination of a high view of Scripture and a careful consideration of literary tools.

Leland and Philip Graham Ryken have a very helpful introduction to the use of literary approaches to the Bible in the opening of their *ESV Literary Study Bible*, where they state emphatically, "It is entirely possible to begin a literary analysis of the Bible exactly where all study of the Bible should begin—by accepting as true all

---

[2] Machiavelli, *The Prince and Selected Discourses,* trans. D. Donno (New York: Bantam, 1966), 84–87.

that the biblical writers say about the Bible (its inspiration by God, its reliability, its complete truthfulness, etc.)."[3]

Studying the metaphors of the Bible is, then, a way of seeking after the meaning of biblical passages. Understanding the literary quality of the passages will allow us to avoid errors of interpretation that sometimes accompany an overly literal reading of the text. For example, in John 10:9, Christ said, "I am the door." He did not mean, literally, that he was a plank but rather that he was a means of access, a metaphorical rendering made clear in the rest of the verse, "If anyone enters by Me, he will be saved and will come in and go out and find pasture," and which is consistent with the panorama of biblical revelation about Christ.

Metaphors are particularly important when we talk about God because any attempt to discuss God in human terms is always a dicey enterprise. How do we translate the infinite into the realm of the finite? How can created beings wrap their minds around the inconceivable nature of the divine? For humans to conceive of God, we must use pictures or images that help us understand the nature of God. Since God is the Creator of the universe and stands beyond the physical world, it is impossible for us to describe Him accurately and completely. He is infinite and, as such, cannot be condensed into simple terms.

The carefully wrought poetry of the Puritan divine Edward Taylor, which was collected in the single work *Christographia*, explored the nature of God. Central to his explorations was the mystically charged notion of somehow translating the Word made Flesh back into Word again, even if it is through poetic words. For Taylor, "metaphors and metaphorical language create a system for understanding reality. Metaphors are part of reality. They are . . . vehicles which carry truth."[4] As Taylor indicated, the incarnation changed the way that we understand God, for the revelation we received in the Hebrew Scriptures was changed in

---

[3] L. and P. G. Ryken, *ESV Literary Study Bible* (Wheaton: Crossway, 2007), xiii.
[4] D. G. Miller, *The Word Made Flesh Made Word: The Failure and Redemption of Metaphor in Edward Taylor's* Christographia (Selinsgrove, PA: Susquehanna University Press, 1995), 26.

incredible ways when interpreted in the light of the incarnation itself. Through the New Testament's record of the incarnation, we have new information that helps us understand God's redemptive plan in history. No longer are we dependent on metaphor alone: we have Christ Himself to provide us with concrete insights into God's nature.

The incarnation, however, also is filled with metaphors. John's Gospel records a number of metaphors that Christ Himself employed to communicate His nature: Bread of Life (6:35), Light of the world (8:12), Gate for the sheep (10:7), Good Shepherd (10:11), the Way, the Truth, and the Life (14:6), and the True Vine (15:1). Each of these helps us to conceptualize beyond the literal personhood of Christ and to approach the overall sense of how His Person applied His qualities. For example, Christ instructed us to consider Him to be a Good Shepherd: He loves in the way that a shepherd loves his flock. We are His and He protects us, cares for us, and leads us. In light of this metaphor, Christians read Psalm 23 in ways that Jewish readers do not, precisely because we read that passage through this metaphorical lens. Similarly, while Christ does not call Himself "Redeemer" in the Gospels, Christians cannot read the story of Ruth or the declarations about the longed-for redeemer in Job 19:25, Ps 19:14, Isa 41:14, and so many other passages without understanding them in terms of Christ's ultimate fulfillment of the metaphor.

Ironically, metaphors for God (and the Persons of the Trinity) are based on literal conceptions of human roles. God is understood as a father in a literal sense (as the Father of Christ), even as He is conceived of in terms of what we know as the characteristics associated with human fathers ("Our Father, which art in heaven" is metaphorical for humankind). God is viewed as a son in a literal sense (as the Son of God,) even as He is understood in how He functioned as a son in more metaphorical ways (such as in explicit obedience to the Father: "not My will be done, but Thine"). Even in Christ's famous reply to Thomas, "I am the Way, the Truth, and the Life" (John 14:6), He is employing a double level of meaning. He is, according to an orthodox and literal understanding of the statement, the sole path to salvation, the sole source of truth, and the sole means of access to eternal life; further, He is the embodiment of the ultimate metaphorical path ("the way" that leads through life into eternity), the ultimate reality ("the truth" of life's purpose and existence), and the ultimate meaning ("the life" that will never end through grace itself). Christ is a friend, whose role works both literally and metaphorically. God is our Maker, both literally and metaphorically.

Metaphors help us to flesh out abstract ideas. Biblical metaphors about God help us to conceive of His nature in ways that plain description cannot do. For example, when 1 John 4:16 tells us, "And we have come to know and to believe the love that God has for us. God is love, and the one who remains in love remains in God, and God remains in him." If we are to apply this conception, to ask how to remain in love and in God, then we find images of this kind of love through the metaphors that the Bible provides. We love like a father, like a son, like a brother, like a shepherd, like a kinsman redeemer, and so forth.

Metaphors gain special power when we ourselves have an intersection with the concept. For example, before I became a father, my understanding of God the Father was limited by my personal experiences to the realm of how I as a son have related to my own father. When I held my own children for the first time, when they took their first steps, when they laugh or cry, and when I discipline them, I understand in new ways the joy and pride that God the Father takes in us, as well as the sorrow that He feels when we choose to be disobedient. My conception of God is enhanced by my own participation with the metaphor.

Metaphors, then, do not circumscribe our understanding of God, but rather are an open door to understanding that our finite conceptions of God are only a crack in the door through which we peer into the vastness of God's nature. Metaphors are a dim glass, to be sure, but they do give us a glimpse. As long as we do not seek to define God through metaphors, they are valuable aids to understanding.

The metaphors that Christ uses in John are instructive on another level as well, in that they are an example of God (in the Second Person of the Trinity) revealing Himself through metaphors. While Christ does this in His sermons, the Scriptures, as divinely inspired, do this throughout the Bible itself. God is, to cite a few examples, Judge (Gen 18:25), Warrior (Exod 15:3), Potter (Isa 64:8), and even Architect (Heb 11:10). Each of these images gives us another insight into how God's relationship with His creation plays out. One metaphor stands out in my mind: that of God as Author.

God as Author

Many years ago, in a freshman composition course, I was working with my students to help them learn the in's and out's of the Modern Language Association style guide for documentation. One of the course requirements was a long research paper on a contemporary issue.

I required a wide variety of sources for the papers, which meant that I was asked a ton of questions about proper documentation details. One day I had sort of reached my limit, and I stopped listening carefully. I finally said in exasperation, "Look everyone, it's not that hard. It's author-title-publishing source-date as the basic entry. All of the variations are built on that model. If it doesn't make sense, just look it up in your book! Use a little initiative! And remember, in your paper's parenthetical notes, just put the author's name and the page number. Author-page number. Keep it simple!"

When the papers stacked up on the due date, I started working my way through them, marking them up carefully to determine the appropriate grade. As any teacher will tell you, the highlight of grading is the comic relief that an occasional gaffe will provide. One paper in that stack caught my eye and still stands out in my memory.

Because I was teaching at a Christian college, many of my students used Scripture as a resource for their examinations of the issues. When I graded one paper, I found that the student had cited a long passage from Romans and in the parenthetical reference, put down the author and the page number: (Holy Spirit 1331).

That citation revealed both the student's high view of Scripture and an allusion to one of the great but underappreciated biblical metaphors for God: Author. In the same way that I love the concept of God as Father because I am a father, my career as a writer gives me a special affinity for this metaphor.

In the Scriptures, God is not presented only as a metaphorical author. Oddly enough, He is presumed to be literate. Certainly, Christ was literate (he reads in Luke 4:17 and writes in John 8:6), but even beyond the Second Person of the Trinity, God writes.

When I was a child, I always looked forward to the annual Easter weekend showing of *The Ten Commandments*, that wonderfully schmaltzy Charlton Heston showcase. One scene in particular always captured my imagination: the carving of the Ten Commandments themselves, by God Himself, through the use of a kind of divine laser engraving action. I am sure that this scene did as much to shape my earliest understandings of divine inspiration and the authority of Scripture as did anything else. The film's effects convey the image of Exod 31:18, "[God] gave him the two tablets of the testimony, stone tablets inscribed by the finger of God." God Himself, then, has the ability to write out His communiqués with humankind.

The finger of God may be extended into the hand of God in Daniel 5, when a mysterious hand writes on the wall of Belshazzar's palace. While the text specifically says that the hand was "a man's," clearly it was a hand that was guided by God, with words that were divinely chosen to prophesy the death of the king.

God is a literal writer, but in several passages, He is described more appropriately through metaphorical status. When Eph 2:10 calls Christians God's "creation" (HCSB) or "workmanship" (KJV and most others), the Greek term is *poiēma*, the word from which we derive the English "poetry." There is a strong sense of authorship to that passage that becomes clearer in the light of other passages that link together God's creative agency with images of authorship.

In the English speaking world, the most notorious use of the term "author" is in the King James translation of Heb 12:2, where Jesus is termed "the author and finisher of our faith." The term that is translated is *archēgon*, which is translated in many English language versions as "author" but really has more of the sense of "creator," which is reflected in its translation as "source" (HCSB) or "founder" (ESV). These translations probably match the term *teleiotēs*, which carries the sense of fulfilling the creative agency through perfect completion.

For the ancients, authorship was tied directly with divine creation. Our modern concept of an author as a generator of narrative is far removed from the classical understanding of the term. Prior to the Enlightenment, authorship was understood in terms of mimesis, the emulation of ideas that were divinely oriented and connected directly with the metaphysical realm. Authors were "inspired" by the muses, the Volva (of the Norse), the Apsaras (of classical India), or other supernatural figures. They tapped into a divine source of insight, a source that held specific authority over the ideas as expressions of divine thoughts. Authors, then, were conduits, not creators, but they were connected with the ultimate metaphysical source of their inspiration, the ultimate Author.

Authors, then, held a kind of extended divine authority over their stories, an authority that the audience respected gravely. Even for the pagans, this authority was a cosmologically powerful concept because it carried an ethical function: narrative helped humans know what was right and how they might live in accordance with such ideals.

This moral force of authorship is connected directly with the Author-Creator metaphor of Scripture. In Rom 2:15, where Paul discusses how God's revelation of Himself outside of the Scriptures holds all persons accountable before Him, he notes that "they show that the work of the law is written on their hearts." This image picks back up on that of Exod 31:18, echoing the idea that God's finger wrote not only on the stone tablets but also on the very hearts of humankind. His story is written, in some way at least, on our very hearts such that we recognize the laws that

He has revealed throughout the universe. This connection between God as Author and God as Creator clarifies what Paul said in Rom 1:18–20:

> For God's wrath is revealed from heaven against all godlessness and unrighteousness of people who by their unrighteousness suppress the truth, since what can be known about God is evident among them, because God has shown it to them. For His invisible attributes, that is, His eternal power and divine nature, have been clearly seen since the creation of the world, being understood through what He has made. As a result, people are without excuse.

One unfortunate result of the Enlightenment is our tendency to create intellectual silos that separate concepts from one another. In our drive to create taxonomies of everything, we have generated artificial distinctions between concepts that cannot and, indeed, should not be completely distinct. In the area of theology, this happens with some frequency as well, such that, in this case, the doctrines of inspiration and creation are held at arm's length from one another so that we lose sight of the reality that there is a seamless overlapping between the two concepts. God's revelation of Himself through inspiration is related directly to His creative agency over the world, and His creative agency expresses itself through His self-revelation.

In systematic theology, the idea that God has revealed Himself in His creation is called "general revelation," and it is critical to understanding how God has communicated His nature to humankind across cultures and millennia. I will return to the concept of general revelation shortly, but for now, suffice it to say that the scope of God's authorship is grand, to say the least.

The connection between the Author and Creator, though, runs much deeper in terms of how it plays out in God's relationship with His handiwork. If God is a distant Creator who simply served as a First Cause to a chain of events, then He has no personal link to His creation. If, however, God is personal Author-Creator, then we can look to the attributes of an author to gain a glimpse of how personal He is as a creator.

Reconsidering Authorship

As I indicated previously, when I became a father, I completely overhauled my understanding about the metaphor of God as Father. No longer was "father" an abstraction for me; it was very real and very instructive in how I might think of God's love for me. I have had a similar experience when I consider the metaphor of God as Author.

As a writer, I have found that my relationship with the narratives that I produce provides me with a fresh appreciation for God's role as Author-Creator. I often joke that one of the benefits of the writing process is that writers get to experience a small taste of what it might be like to be gods. Artists in general share this role: when they are creating art, they are godlike in their creative agency. Writers can create characters, alter the laws of physics, and can cause death and destruction. Writers have all but absolute power in the worlds that they create.[5] Because of this, authorship helps us to understand in a very small way these ideas about the nature of God.

* *God Is Outside the Story:* When writers generate narrative, they usually take great care to craft the story in ways that provide clues to the audience about not only what is happening in the plot but also what might happen. We call this foreshadowing, the deliberate providing of clues to the story. As the audience notes these clues, a sense of suspense or irony can develop, where the audience begins

---

[5] This is, perhaps, one of the reasons that so many artists succumb to addictive pathologies. When their writing sessions are over for the day, they must reenter the real world, where trash must be carried to the curb, where bills must be paid, where spouses and children must be engaged. The shift is jarring, and it often leads to alcoholism and other dependencies. The burden of being a god, even a metaphorical god, is too great for human shoulders.

to guess what will happen. In effective fiction, the author then undercuts these presumptions in ways that add surprise to their reading.

Foreshadowing is possible precisely because authors are external to their stories. They may allow the story to unfold organically, but in the editing process, authors have the ability to step outside of the timeline of their stories to affect these kinds of insights, breaking into the story as it develops in order to shape the action.

Similarly, authors can step into the story to intervene in its action.[6] They are not bound by the usual parameters of time and space. They can rearrange events, add new events, add new characters, or even take away persons who ultimately affect the outcome of the story.

Because God generates the story, He has a perspective that the characters within the story cannot share. He knows the story's events in advance. He can shift the development of the events in ways that determine their outcome in support of His overall purposes for the story. In this light, we understand God's sovereignty in new ways. Prophecy takes on a new meaning as we understand that God's perspective on history is not ours. The Scriptures use both "predestination" and "foreknowledge" to describe God's role in history (in the same verse, actually, Rom 8:29), and however we deal with the tension between human free will and God's sovereignty, the bottom line is that in either case, God is outside of the time line of history and enjoys authority over it.

---

[6] One of the great debates in creative writing theory is whether or not narratives should be plot-driven or character-driven. I side with the latter, but one of the great challenges of creating character-driven narrative is that of manipulating the plot in ways that force even fictional characters to react to the changes. If nothing else, good writing tends to create a situation or a challenge at the start of the story, even if it relies solely on characters to meet the challenge. In this way, the author's use of plot to set up the characters' developments is consistent with even character-driven narrative.

*   *God Tells the Truth:* Even though much of narrative is fictional, it is not untruthful. The best stories tell truths through imaginative means. In fact, one of the foremost commands that teachers of fiction writing provide to their students is that of remaining faithful to truth telling. Anne Lamott ties this in with the author's voice: "And the truth of your experience can *only* come through in your own voice. If it is wrapped in someone else's voice, we readers will feel suspicious, as if you are dressed up in someone else's clothes. . . . Truth, or reality, or whatever you want to call it is the bedrock of life."[7] Booker T. Washington indicated that he felt a moral imperative to tell the truth in all that he communicated with his audiences: "I was determined to say nothing that I did not feel from the bottom of my heart to be true and right."[8]

Truth telling in narrative is difficult to separate from its imaginative nature, for a good story is rarely journalistically or historically accurate.[9] Characters are invented, events are synthesized, and themes are imposed. In most narrative, truth and imagination are not mutually exclusive concepts.[10]

When an author lies to the audience, though, it disrupts the bonds of trust that have been created by the relationship. Sometimes an author will mislead the audience in

---

[7] A. Lamott, *Bird by Bird: Some Instructions on Writing and Life* (New York: Anchor, 1994), 199–200.

[8] B. T. Washington, *Up from Slavery* (New York: Dover, 1995), 102.

[9] Christian readers in particular often have a hard time finding this line between imagination and truthfulness. Indeed, I once had a creative writing student who asked if he needed to confess the "lies" he told in his fiction. What is more, there are hermeneutical questions related to biblical text that may be raised by the idea that the Bible itself contains narrative. Among these questions is this, "If you are saying that fictional narratives can communicate truth, then are you saying that the Bible can be truthful but still not be literally true?" I am not saying that at all. In all cases, the text is trustworthy. This is because God always tells the truth.

[10] I should hasten to make clear, however, that I am not saying that accuracy is not an important part of fiction writing. If there were any lesson that should be gleaned from the debacle of D. Brown's *The Da Vinci Code*, it is that errors of fact (egregious ones, in Brown's case) irreparably mar fiction.

order to effect certain responses or even to manipulate audience perceptions (such as in the use of red herrings in detective fiction), but these are not lies in the sense of being moral falsehoods; they are tricks used to heighten audience involvement.

One of the challenges to authorial truthfulness is that of stepping beyond the author's own personal boundaries. I rarely write stories with female protagonists because try as I might, as a male I have difficulty generating female characters who ring "true." Nothing is worse than reading a story written by someone whose ignorance has unintentionally produced cringingly poor representations of a subject or a character.

For God, the stakes are even higher in that He is an Author who is revealing Himself to the world. He is not spinning a purely imaginary story to make a purely imaginary point. He is creating a narrative that reveals His own nature. By reading His story, we are able to comprehend Him. This creates a genuine need for Him to tell the truth at every turn, for by these truths we are able to know and relate to Him.

The Scriptures link God and truth at every turn, emphasizing the notion that God's truth is real truth, the kind that we long for and that stands whether we recognize it or not. Psalm 25:5 says, "Guide me in Your truth and teach me, for You are the God of my salvation; I wait for You all day long." A few verses later, the psalmist declares, "All the LORD's ways show faithful love and truth to those who keep His covenant and decrees" (v. 10). God's truth is linked inextricably to His faithful, constant love in several other psalms (Pss 26:3, 40:10–11; 57:3; 61:7; 85:10, 89:14; and 115:1). It guides us (43:3), and it rises out of the earth, even as righteousness looks down from heaven (85:11).

God's truth transcends human experience, standing apart from our evaluation of it; whether we accept it (and its applications) or not, it persists as truth. This is foundational to Paul's exposition in the opening of Rom 1:18–25:

> For God's wrath is revealed from heaven against all godlessness and unrighteousness of people who by their unrighteousness suppress the truth, since what can be known about God is evident among them, because God has shown it to them. For His invisible attributes, that is, His eternal power and divine nature, have been clearly seen since the creation of the world, being understood through what He has made. As a result, people are without excuse. For though they knew God, they did not glorify Him as God or show gratitude. Instead, their thinking became nonsense, and their senseless minds were darkened. Claiming to be wise, they became fools and exchanged the glory of the immortal God for images resembling mortal man, birds, four-footed animals, and reptiles. Therefore God delivered them over in the cravings of their hearts to sexual impurity, so that their bodies were degraded among themselves. They exchanged the truth of God for a lie, and worshiped and served something created instead of the Creator, who is praised forever.

Like God's existence, God's truth does not depend on human affirmation. It transcends anything that is created.

Finally, revealed truth is Christocentric. Christ called Himself "the way, the truth, and the life" as He asserted the uniqueness of His status in the universe (John 14:6). Earlier, John noted that although "the law was given through Moses, grace and truth came through Jesus Christ" (1:17). In Christ, we have the fullest, truest self-revelation of God; all of our understanding of truth is rooted in the nature and person of Christ. Truth is not simply propositional; it is incarnational.

* *God's Story Has a Point*: In a creative writing seminar, one of my students wrote an interesting story that included very beautiful passages that described the setting of the plot. He used beautiful language to convey the tone of the locale, and his characters were drawn well too. When we workshopped the story with the rest of the class, however, the other students noted that the story never seemed to go anywhere. There was no plot arc, only a loosely linked series of descriptive glimpses that never seemed to connect. When I met with the student after class to go over his work, he was upset over the response of his fellow students. "They didn't see what I was trying to do!" he lamented. When I asked him what he had tried to do, he said, "I wanted to show the pointlessness of everything. That despite the beauty that we may find, there is no point. Despite the characters in our own lives, there is no point. Nothing has a point." I chuckled and said, "So your point was that you had no point? Can you identify for me the logical flaw in that thinking?" Begrudgingly, he said he did. "Besides," I continued, "you are cheating your readers. By telling your story, by writing it, you have entered into a tacit agreement with your audience that you will not waste their time. You will have something to say. They will learn something or at least feel something as they read it, or they will feel cheated. It's almost as though we get to the end of your story, and you say, 'Psych! Fooled you!' That's not very nice."

Young writers who are under the spell of philosophy or criticism often succumb to such a temptation, but experienced writers, and especially working professional writers of narrative, know that there must be a point to a story or else we are left with a rambling tale that ends up making the audience feel as though it is stuck viewing a stranger's slides of a vacation to Mexico. Such narrative is a little like Macbeth's comment about the emptiness of life: "It is a tale told by an idiot, full of sound and fury, signifying nothing" (5.5.26–27).[11] In his famous acceptance speech upon receiving the 1949 Nobel Prize in Literature, William Faulkner noted that the highest goal for writing is the detailing of "the problems of the human heart in conflict with itself which alone can make good writing because only that is worth writing about, worth the agony and the sweat."[12] Faulkner's most important novel, *The Sound and the Fury,* took its title from that passage in Macbeth; his novels' themes underscore the importance of writing narratives that do *not* become meaningless tales told by idiots.

Authors seek to reveal some kind of insight, typically some sort of truth, which allows their audience the opportunity to experience the power of enlightenment in some way. Whether it is a life's narrative, such as that of Frederick Douglass[13] or Mark Mathabane,[14] or cultural criticism like Albert Camus's *The Stranger,*[15] or even Moliere's *Tartuffe,*[16] authors have a point they are conveying. This point guides the way that they select genres, character development, settings, and any range of the narrative's details; in short, the author's point governs almost everything else about the narrative.[17]

[11] W. Shakespeare, *Macbeth,* in *The Riverside Shakespeare* (Dallas: Houghton Mifflin, 1974).
[12] W. Faulkner, "Banquet Speech (December 10, 1950)," in *Nobel Lectures, Literature 1901–1967,* ed. Horst Frenz (Amsterdam: Elsevier Publishing Company, 1969). Posted at http://nobelprize.org/nobel_prizes/literature/laureates/1949/faulkner-speech.html; accessed April 22, 2009.
[13] F. Douglass, *Narrative of the Life of Frederick Douglass* (1845; repr., New York: Dover, 1995).
[14] M. Mathabane, *Kaffir Boy: An Autobiography; The True Story of a Black Youth's Coming of Age in Apartheid South Africa* (New York: Free Press, 1998).
[15] A. Camus, *The Stranger,* trans. S. Gilbert (New York: Vintage, 1946).
[16] Moliere, *Tartuffe,* trans. P. L. Steiner (Indianapolis: Hackett, 2008).
[17] I realize, of course, that literary critics will immediately ask, "So how do we know what the author's point is?" as well as a related question, "How many points does a story have?" This is the principle of the intentional fallacy, which

In the case of God, His point is the revelation of Himself to His creation. Through general revelation, God tells His story in ways that reveal His authority, His righteousness, and His faithfulness. Through special revelation, God tells His story in ways that provide further details to the elements of His nature, using the nation of Israel as a primary platform in the Old Testament and the fulfillment of the incarnation and Christ's ministry of grace in the New Testament. To some extent, His point is crystallized in the *shema* of Deut 6:4 ("Listen, Israel: Yahweh our God, Yahweh is One. Love the LORD your God with all your heart, with all your soul, and with all your strength"), and it is applied in Lev 19:18 ("Love your neighbor as yourself.)" As Christ Himself noted in Matt 22:40, "All the Law and the Prophets depend on these two commandments."

* *God Loves His Characters:* Authors develop relationships with the characters who populate their narrative. Some of the relationships are benign and passive; some are deep and emotional. To some extent this is a function of the way that a narrative's plot unfolds. Some characters are flat and stereotypical, conveying little personality, and others are round and vibrant, almost living beings of their own.

As a fiction writer myself, I can attest to how an author can develop an incredibly loving relationship with a character, especially a primary character who continues through a

---

is widely employed in contemporary literary criticism. Most producers of narrative, however, do not buy into the concept of the intentional fallacy on the same scale as do critics of narrative. Most writers will readily agree that multiple meanings may be found in a work, even, perhaps, meanings that the author had not previously noted (I have experienced this myself; the author's subconscious should never be underestimated!), but most will also assert that the author is the correct locus for the *primary* meaning. Stanley Fish famously claimed that reading communities determine the meaning of texts in *Is There a Text in This Class: The Authority of Interpretive Communities* (Boston: Harvard University Press, 1982). Even among literary critics, Fish's arguments are seen as an extreme when taken to their nth degree. *My* point is that authors intend to have a point, one that is perceivable in good writing.

number of stories. Some years ago, I wrote about a character, Danny, whom I adored. He was a sweet, polite little boy who was that clean-faced, innocent child that everyone knows from somewhere and who, in this case, was trapped in a home with an abusive, alcoholic father. As the story unfolded, I began to realize that in order to be true to what I was communicating, Danny was going to have to die in an accident. There was no way that his nature as a tragic figure would allow him to survive. I tried to think through a hundred alternate scenarios that could avoid it. I even thought about leaving the story unfinished, but that felt wrong as well. Typing in that scene was one of the hardest things I have ever done in my life. I could smell the dust and the blood as the scene came to my mind. I could hear his mother's moaning sobs. In some ways, I felt as though I were writing about the death of my own child. It moved me deeply: I cried the entire time and was depressed for a week. I loved that little boy as any father would.

William Faulkner felt that way about one of his main characters, Caddy Compson, who appears in several novels and stories, notably *The Sound and the Fury.* Faulkner noted in hindsight that he loved her character, in spite of the troubled life (and temperament!) she would carry into the future. Faulkner himself called Caddy his "heart's darling."[18] One scene in particular held his ardor throughout his writing of her character, an early one when she was very young and was climbing a tree with her brothers, with a smear of mud on her bottom. He noted in a later introduction to *The Sound & the Fury* that the scene was "perhaps the only thing in literature which would ever move me very much."[19]

---

[18] W. Faulkner, *Faulkner in the University: Class Conferences at the University of Virginia 1957–1958,* ed. Frederick L. Gwynn and Joseph L. Blotner (Charlottesville, VA: University of Virginia Press, 1959), 6.

[19] W. Faulkner, "An Introduction for *The Sound and the Fury,*" unpublished 1933 version in *The Southern Review* (1972): 8; pp. 705–710; reproduced at

God's love for humankind, the living breathing "characters" who populate history, is emblematic of His nature. We are His well-crafted *poiēma*, whose own nature reflects His.[20] As 1 John 4:19 notes, "We love because He first loved us." His plan of salvation for humankind has been His plan since "before the earth's foundation" (John 17:24; Eph 1:4; and Rev 13:8). God's love for us is crucial, then, to how we view His redemptive story as a whole, for it is best interpreted through the lens of the incarnation: "But God proves His own love for us in that while we were still sinners Christ died for us!" (Rom 5:8). God's loving attachment to His creation is powerful and deeply set.

As Author, then, God has a Story to tell. He has a point to make. He wishes to communicate with His intended audience, the entirety of humankind. He reveals His Story to us through a variety of modes, each of which has a specific effectiveness.

Authorship and General Revelation

For centuries, theologians have called God the Author of not one but two books, the Book of God (the Bible) and the Book of Nature (His creation). Galileo, for example, believed that God employed mathematics as the language of the Book of Nature. The notion of God's two books reflects the way that the doctrine of revelation is articulated throughout much of Christian history.

Because humankind is finite, God's revelation of Himself is a mystery. In fact, this revelation requires a level of sophistication

---

"Faulkner's Introductions to *The Sound and the Fury*," http://www.usask.ca/english/faulkner/main/intros1933/index.html (accessed May 2, 2009).

[20] I do not wish to wade into the arguments about free will and God's sovereignty, but I must insert an observation that any writer of narrative can affirm: while the author creates characters and crafts them within the boundaries of the work, characters are amazingly vibrant and surprising creations, sometimes frustratingly assertive of their own personalities. In saying that human authors are imperfect in their knowledge of characters, I am not asserting the same for God, which is to say that I am not an open theist in any way. My observations about characters in this section are rooted in the author's attachment to them. I will leave discourses on the nature of these characters to others.

and delicacy that could only be designed by an infinite Person. As Millard J. Erickson has termed it, "Because man is finite and God is infinite, if man is to know God it must come about by God's revelation of himself to man. By this we mean God's manifestation of himself to man in such a way that man can know and fellowship with him."[21] God's plan for self-revelation is indeed ingenious. Through general revelation of Himself in the created world, His being and nature may be observed. Through special revelation in Scripture, His redemptive mission is detailed through a specific platform of His relationship with Israel. Finally, God's self-revelation was made most complete through the incarnation, when He Himself condescended to live among men as the Second Person of the Trinity: Christ.

Systematic theology prioritizes these modes of revelation in terms of their relative authority, making general revelation subject to special revelation and special revelation, to the incarnation. Other theological approaches may alter such a hierarchy; notably, narrative theology tends to prioritize general revelation over (and sometimes against) special revelation, emphasizing the narrative content even of the Bible in ways that draw more precisely on principles associated with general revelation. For those who take a systematic approach, however, the hierarchy of interpretive authority is critical to a consistent and cogent understanding of God's self-revelation.

General revelation may be noted in three dominant places: "nature, history, and the constitution of the human being."[22] Nature reflects God's attention to orderliness and even the very act of self-revelation (the very discoverability of nature, our ability to analyze and discover the world around us). History reveals God's teleological (guided) hand in bringing all events to the ultimate reconciliation of the world under the Lordship of Christ. Human experiences provide us with glimpses of God's character. Each of these elements opens the door to our perceptions ever so slightly. Further, general revelation is general in "its universal

---

[21] M. J. Erickson, *Christian Theology* (Grand Rapids: Baker, 1985), 153.
[22] Ibid., 154.

availability (it is accessible to all persons at all times) and the content of the message (it is less particularized and detailed than special revelation)."[23]

General revelation is helpful in understanding how God reveals Himself more broadly throughout human history. As Erickson observes, "At least in theory something can be learned from the study of God's creation. General revelation will be of value when it sheds light upon the special revelation or fills it out at certain points where it does not speak."[24] General revelation, however, suffers from two distinct handicaps: one, who determines what qualifies as an example of general revelation, and, two, how can we reconcile general revelation with special revelation when they often are complementary rather than corresponding? Orthodox theology always places general revelation in a position of submission to special revelation.[25] Erickson underscores these problems in this way: "We need to be careful in our correlation of theology and other disciplines [science, psychology, etc.], however. While the special revelation (preserved for us in the Bible) and the general revelation are ultimately in harmony with one another, that harmony is apparent only as each is fully understood and correctly interpreted."[26]

This is the literal meaning behind DeYoung and Kluck's parable of the elephant and the blind men that I mentioned in the chapter 1. To some extent, general revelation allows the blind men access to the elephant with senses that are limited. General revelation is difficult business to employ to develop specific answers to questions about God's nature. In special revelation, however, the elephant speaks and declares, "I am an elephant!" What is more, in the incarnation, the blind men receive sight and see the elephant clearly with their own eyes.

The first few chapters of Romans are foundational to the Christian understanding of concepts such as natural law, the idea

---

[23] Ibid.

[24] Erickson, *Christian Theology,* 72.

[25] In this way, then, the doctrines of Revelation and Inspiration are linked inextricably.

[26] Erickson, *Christian Theology,* 72–73.

that the world contains universal moral principles that may be discerned. Classic texts such as *Written on Their Hearts*[27] and *Making Men Moral*[28] explored natural law in ways that are beyond the scope of the present work, but the *gravitas* of Paul's phrasing is extensive.

Indeed, C. S. Lewis found this to be central to his concept of Tao as outlined in *The Abolition of Man*. For Lewis, this principle may be discovered not only in our psychological makeup, but in the great texts of humankind as well. At the conclusion of *Abolition*, he included a compilation and comparison of these works.[29]

I should mention that despite the subordination of general revelation to special revelation, there are times when it may give us insight into the Scriptures themselves. This should not surprise us because God designed both in service to His self-revelation. When we see God as the Rock of our salvation (Ps 89:26), we can go back to nature and learn about rocks and bring those insights back to amplify the Scripture. Then we can understand new dimensions to Christ's observations about the two men who built their respective houses on sand and rock (Matt 7:24–26). A little knowledge of geology will be helpful in enhancing our interpretation of such passages. The locus of authority in the interpretation is in the Scripture itself, but that authority is enhanced by our understanding of general revelation.

The subordination of general revelation to special revelation provides, I think, a helpful model for the relationship between narrative theology and systematic theology. In the last couple of decades, a movement developed, sometimes called post-liberal theology, which included a prioritization of narrative approaches over (and often against) systematic theology. Truth may be determined through narrative, but that truth is always consistent with its overall portrayal in the entirety of special revelation. When narrative

[27] J. Budziszewski, *Written on Their Hearts: The Case for Natural Law* (Downers Grove: IVP, 1997).
[28] R. P. George, *Making Men Moral: Civil Liberties and Public Morality* (New York: Oxford University Press, 1995).
[29] C. S. Lewis, "Illustrations of the *Tao*," in *The Abolition of Man* (New York: HarperSanFransisco, 1974), 83–101.

theology isolates the Bible's narratives into independent units, it errs by approaching the Scriptures as lacking overall integrity. When narrative theology ignores the theological consistencies of Scripture, it conflicts with the lessons of history. When narrative theology subordinates revealed truth to abstract relationship, then it perpetuates an understanding of the Bible that is shortsighted.[30] Further, narrative is a vehicle for the application of theological concepts, but systematic theology provides a clear roadway for that vehicle. Systematic theology maintains order and a consistent trajectory; narrative theology makes systematic theology useful by moving people down the road toward their ultimate goal: understanding and glorifying God. Neither functions effectively without the other.[31]

The ability of general revelation to inform special revelation is important as well because we need to remember that general revelation is a powerful, God-designed force. We tend to de-fang it into a mushy "good feeling about the universe," filled with sort of glorified Ziggy cartoon moments of applauding beautiful sunsets and shouting, "Go God!" We would do well to remember, however, that the Scripture passages used to support general revelation are not passive but rather aggressive in their portrayals of God's self-revelation. Psalm 19:1 indicates that the heavens "declare" and the sky "proclaims" God's glory and the work of His hands. It does not say, "God's glory and the work of His hands may be discovered in the heavens and the sky." God's self-revelation is not the result of human reason's work of discovery. Humans, enabled

---

[30] On the whole, the major proponents of narrative theology link it with systematic theology in some ways, including using narrative theology as a means of developing a strong systematic theology. The misuse of it comes more significantly in the ways that it is applied by secondary scholars and writers. For more information on narrative theology, see R. Alter's *The Art of Biblical Narrative* (New York: Basic Books, 1983); S. Hauerwas's *A Community of Character: Toward a Constructive Christian Social Ethic* (South Bend: University of Notre Dame Press, 1981); and M. Goldberg's *Theology and Narrative: A Critical Introduction* (Eugene: Wipf and Stock, 2001).

[31] A recent fiction blockbuster is an example of how elevating narrative theology over systematic theology can produce a mixture of both emotionally charged fiction and poorly conceived theology: W. P. Young's *The Shack* (Los Angeles: Windblown, 2007), which I will discuss further in chapter eight. Likewise, systematic theology without narrative elements produces poorly connected abstractions, a concept I will discuss in chapter seven.

by the Holy Spirit, join in the process of general revelation; they do not generate it. This underscores the importance of special revelation as a guide to general revelation, as it was likewise guided by the inspiration of the Holy Spirit.

God, then, is not just the Author of the Gospel or even the Scriptures. He is the Author-Creator of the material world, the realm of human experience. What's more, He is the Author of the incarnation, which stands as the key for the right interpretation of both special and general revelation. The scope of the craft of His authorship is all but inconceivable.

Inverting the Author/Story Metaphor

When we consider metaphors for God, we usually begin with the process of exploring how God is like a metaphorical comparison: God is like a loving father in that He loves His children sacrificially and unconditionally, He rejoices in His children, and He longs to be reconciled with those who have estranged themselves from Him. God is the "tenor" of the metaphor, and "father" is the vehicle of the comparison. In other metaphors, "Christ" is the tenor of the metaphor, and "shepherd" is the vehicle. In others, "Christ" is the tenor, and "king" is the vehicle.

The Christian consideration of these metaphors does not stop with these conceptions, however, for we often will invert these roles and use God not as the tenor of the metaphor but rather as the vehicle of an idealized form of the tenor. What I mean is that because we conceive of God as a father, we are justified in considering how fathers should be godly in how they emulate the love of God. We may consider what a Christlike shepherd (usually converted to "pastor," based on Eph 4:11) may do. We may ponder how a Christly king may rule in his sphere.

Such inverse comparisons are valid because we view God as the source of all idealized attributes and actions, and they are helpful in applying the metaphors to real life. I know that as a father, I look to my heavenly Father for examples of how I might improve my application of the responsibilities I have. I do not consider how a father might be a god, but rather how a father might be god-*ly*. I want my home to depict what God has revealed a godly home to be. I want to invert the metaphor in my own life.

Because we conceive of the gospel as a story so naturally, it is hardly shocking to think of God as Author. As we have seen, there are Scriptural foundations for this metaphor, but beyond that, something in our minds has so deeply connected gospel with story that it is hard to think of it as anything else. We give testimonies of God's work in our lives that reflect the narrative of God's love toward us. We sing songs about the "old, old story." It is hard not to think of gospel as the tenor of the metaphor and story as the vehicle, just as it is hard not to think of God as the tenor and Author as the vehicle.

What happens, however, when we reverse the roles as we do so naturally with Father, Shepherd, and King? What would it look like if God and gospel became the vehicles and author and story became the tenors? What if our stories contained echoes of God's general revelation of His gospel, of creation–fall–redemption? What if God's authorial role in the universe could provide a hermeneutical key to interpreting human narrative?

If this hermeneutical key exists, then there are important ramifications for how we may read and how we may approach the generation of narrative. If it exists, then there may be fresh understandings of old stories. If it exists, then we may notice full moons in autumn daylight skies that we have never before noted.

3

What Does God's Story Look Like?

The heavens declare the glory of
God, and the sky proclaims the work
of His hands. Day after day they
pour out speech; night after night
they communicate knowledge. There is
no speech; there are no words; their
voice is not heard. Their message
has gone out to all the earth,
and their words to the ends of the
world.

—Psalm 19:1-4

Say first, for Heav'n hides nothing
    from thy view
Nor the deep Tract of Hell, say first
    what cause
Mov'd our Grand Parents in that happy
    State,
Favour'd of Heav'n so highly, to fall
    off
From thir [sic] Creator, and
    transgress his Will
For one restraint, Lords of the World
    besides?

—John Milton, _Paradise Lost_ (1667)
            Book 1, lines 27-32

Twentieth-century author F. Scott Fitzgerald was obsessed with the past. In particular, he constantly focused on his failed relationships with women, most notably the relationship he had with his wife, Zelda Sayre. Fitzgerald had pursued Zelda for years as he sought to establish himself as a writer, only to be rejected by her time after time until he finally sold his first novel, *This Side of Paradise*. Zelda finally gave in and agreed to marry him. Their relationship thereafter was one of constant emotional manipulation and disappointment. Fitzgerald's fiction often reflects his own story, one of heartache, bourgeois pretensions, and women whose presence undermines the successes of men. To some extent, it is as though he tells one story over and over: his own.

I could make a similar point about most fiction writers: in many if not most of their cases, either they tell their own story or the story of their times consistently throughout their works. They make the same points, reuse the same character types, and retell the same events, each time through a slightly different narrative filter. Some critics, called biographical critics, even spend their careers tracing out authors' life events as expressed in their creative work.

When evangelical apologists approach the biblical text, they see God's story expressing itself through a grid, a dominant paradigm that progresses from creation to fall to redemption (I'll return later to a fourth stage, generally called "consummation," "restoration," or "mission"). A Christian worldview builds on all three of these elements, and any worldview that deletes one of the elements is not a fully functioning worldview. Each stage is critical to understanding both the other two stages and to understanding God's redemptive story as a whole. As Charles Colson and Nancy Pearcey have written, "Equipped with this understanding, we can show not only that the Christian worldview gives the best answers—answers that accord with common sense and the most advanced science—but also that Christians can take up spiritual arms in the great cosmic struggle between conflicting worldviews."[1]

---

[1] C. Colson and N. Pearcey, *How Now Shall We Live?* (Wheaton: Tyndale House, 1999), 37.

A Christian worldview begins like any other pursuit by a believer: in a position of humility before a Holy God. By His light, then, we move toward our pursuit. In the case of approaching special revelation in particular, we join in His self-revelation, seeking after His glorification. As David S. Dockery has noted,

> The starting point for a Christian worldview brings us into the presence of God without delay. The central affirmation of Scripture is not only that there is a God but also that God has acted and spoken in history. God is Lord and King over this world, ruling all things for His own glory, displaying His perfections in all that He does in order that humans and angels may worship and adore Him.[2]

Such a starting point helps us see the ultimate lordship of God, through Christ, over all things, including the unity of human knowledge, which is based on a unity of God's self-revelation: "A Christian worldview is not built on various types of truth (religious and philosophical or scientific) but on a universal principle and all-embracing system that shapes religion, natural and social sciences, law, history, health care, the arts, the humanities, and all disciplines of study with application for all of life."[3] All of human understanding is grounded in the singular truth of God's Story.

The creation-fall-redemption framework, then, must reflect the overarching story of the Scripture, the written record of God's self-revelation. Each portion of this framework interlinks with the others, forming a structural concatenation that allows the Story to be followed by its audience.

"Creation," then, explains two salient issues: our origin and our identity. Based on the opening of Genesis, humankind and the rest of the natural world are explained as a part of God's deliberate creative work. The natural world is distinct from, and subject to,

---

[2] D. Dockery, *Renewing Minds: Serving Church and Society through Christian Higher Education* (Nashville: B&H Academic, 2007), 53.
[3] Dockery, *Renewing Minds*, 50–51.

its Creator. The world is not eternal but has a beginning and will have an eventual end. Humankind, in particular, has a distinct relationship with God, which results from His decision to place in us His image. Creation is the opening act of the story, the start of the narrative that reveals God's story. Creation sets the stage for the fall, and the fall would not hold its tragic sense if there were not such a state from which a decline could occur. Creation is perfect, but perfect in a sense of newness, not eternity. It is fragile and can be broken easily. Creation provides an ideal that foreshadows a coming permanence that will occur in the stage of redemption.

"Fall" explains what has gone wrong in the world. Through the sin of Adam and Eve, death came into the world, and chaos along with it. Evil takes root, and human relationships were broken, but more importantly, the relationship between humans and God Himself was disrupted. The delicate balance that had been in place at the creation now shifts out of balance. The fall is especially poignant because of what is lost: harmonious relationships with God, with other persons, and with the natural world. The fall creates the need for a reconciliation, a redemptive act that will restore what was lost.

"Redemption" resolves the problem of the fall, making things right again and restoring the balance that was lost in nature and in relationships. We learn that through Christ, all things are being reconciled to God. We learn that the fallen state of the world is not permanent. We learn that chaos will one day be overwhelmed by grace, and that death itself will expire through the salvific action of Christ.

As a writer, I appreciate the way that the creation-fall-redemption paradigm helps to point to the overarching story of the entirety of the special revelation. Readers tend to fracture the biblical story in ways that disconnect each narrative unit from the remainder of the entire Story. There are many stories contained in the Bible, but there is only one primary Story told by the Bible: that of God's glory as revealed in His justice and loving-kindness toward His creation. Each of the stories it contains contributes to our understanding of the overarching redemptive Story.

This means that the various authors of the biblical record were under the inspiration of a single Author who told the Story. As W. A. Criswell states this, "The more one really studies the Bible the more one is convinced that behind the many authors there is one overruling, controlling mind."[4] This "controlling mind," then, reveals Himself in ways that comprise His Story, that communicate His point to His intended audience, humankind, through special revelation. I am, of course, emphasizing in this way a plenary inspiration to the Scriptures, the idea that the biblical record is fully inspired in its entirety. Erickson states this boldly: "It is our contention here that inspiration involved God's directing the thoughts of the writers, so that they were precisely the thoughts that he wished expressed. At times these thoughts were very specific; at other times they were more general."[5] This approach is typically called the plenary view of inspiration, and it works best as we seek after an expansive understanding of God as Author and the overall unity of His Story.

The creation-fall-redemption paradigm outlines the overarching Story. Through it, we see a fresh unity to special revelation, a unity that reveals a unity of authorship, a concept that is central to the doctrine of Inspiration.

The creation-fall-redemption paradigm is closely linked to God's revelation of Himself in Scripture. It is rooted in Genesis and finds its fulcrum in the incarnation of Christ Himself. It reaches its ultimate consummation in Revelation, as Christ returns to restore His reign in *Jerusalem Celestial*. When we consider the creation-fall-redemption framework, then, as interpretive, we find that it is particularly handy when interpreting the special revelation of Scripture and, thus, Christian theology. It is tied specifically to biblical thought and even biblical language.

Special revelation, then, is at once God's story and God's commentary on His story. When we make the shift to examining God's general revelation, we should expect to find elements that

---

[4] W. A. Criswell, *Why I Preach that the Bible Is Literally True* (Nashville: Broadman Press, 1969), 72.

[5] M. J. Erickson, *Christian Theology* (Grand Rapids: Baker, 1985), 216.

are consistent with His self-revelation in Scripture. This means that we should find echoes of the creation-fall-redemption framework in the natural world, including the human realm.

Reconsidering the Creation-Fall-Redemption Framework

The previous chapter noted the relationship between general and special revelation. As I stated, I prioritize the latter over the former, even as I view both in light of the incarnation. I wonder, however, if this might be an apt analogy to that act: when we look into pure light, we have difficulty adjusting our eyes in such a way as to be able to see in darker fields again. We are, to some extent, dazzled by that perfect light and do not recognize the contours of some of the shadowy areas while our pupils dilate to allow a new focus to occur.

When we employ the language of special revelation, which is biblical language, to describe extrabiblical revelation, then perhaps we are using a light that is too strong to analyze the world of general revelation. What if the terms "creation," "fall," and "redemption" are so tied to the biblical narrative that they blunt our perceptions of general revelation? What if we change the language to describe the principles described in each stage, and then look at general revelation through the lens of terms that are different but faithful to the special revelation terms? Would such a view provide us with a more robust perspective on general revelation?

In this endeavor, we must constantly ensure that we underscore that general revelation is God-revealing in very specific ways because it was God-designed, declaring His glory and His relationship with the universe as its Creator.

Christian thought runs very easily toward employing jargon that is specific to its own community. Anyone who has tried to give his personal testimony of faith to nonbelievers knows how difficult it can be to communicate without using "church" terms. To some extent, we have to learn how to translate from "Christianese" to another language that is understandable to others. In doing this, we are able to communicate the gospel in ways that are faithful and transformative.

I propose that we employ this exercise with the creation-fall-redemption framework in order to discover a more general terminology that might allow us to see just how pervasive this structure is outside the biblical text.

Creation answers the question of our identity and our origins, but more than that, it describes our first state. In Eden, we have a period of initial peace and *shalom*. The newness of the world is untested or unmarred, much like a new car that has just rolled out of a manufacturer's facility. It is a time of robust innocence. It is perfection of a kind that we know, especially in the light of our own experiences, cannot last. It is fragile and delicate. It is beautiful. Creation is a time of balance when conflicts or disturbances have not yet been set into motion in ways that will change everything.

The balance of creation, however, cannot be sustained. We know that the fall will occur because perfection in the material world cannot last, just as innocence cannot be perpetual. Newness and innocence fall into the marring circumstances of experience. When a new car leaves the showroom, its perfection will disappear, and accidents will happen. This imperfection itself is a constant reminder of the loss of perfection, just as imbalance is a reminder of balance lost. The crookedness of imbalance forces a realization that something is lacking, something that we desperately desire but cannot create for ourselves

Redemption restores what was lost. When imbalance occurs, a longing results in which humans crave a renewed sense of balance, just as passengers on a ship rolling in a storm long for the stability that comes from a firm railing. We long for even a temporary sense of stability. When things are desperately out of sorts, we may worry that we cannot find restoration; in fact, sometimes we despair of such hope, but we still seek it. Experience that is purchased from innocence longs for a kind of resolution and sorting of the facts, which allow peace to be rediscovered. Shalom returns as balance is restored. Significantly, Eden is not the land of redemption: heaven is, where there is no fragile perfection. There is no fear of loss or further damage. Because of the redemptive work of Christ, which transcends the physical world, grace restores the balance that had been disrupted.

As I have surveyed possible parallels between creation-fall-redemption and other terms that approximate the principles that stand behind biblical terms, I have been surprised at how many exist. The terms include the triads of perfection, imperfection, and restoration; innocence, experience, and acceptance; peace, conflict, and resolution; and stability, instability, and restoration. Certainly, I have overlooked others, but the more I consider how far-reaching these principles may be, the more convinced I am that general revelation may be much more robust and even theologically pointed than has been presumed heretofore.

For our purposes, I propose that the terminology of "creation," "fall," and "redemption" is parallel to that of "balance," "imbalance," and "restoration." Balance seems to be central to each of the stages, and its loss and subsequent restoration drive a number of interesting insights for our consideration. Eden was a place of balance: natural harmony, relational accord, and peace (shalom). Sin tipped the world out of balance, disrupting the natural order, damaging relational accord, and erasing the peace of the garden and its occupants. This imbalance has echoed throughout the universe, creating a demand for restoration, in nature, between persons, and, most importantly, between God and humankind. Because the loss of balance occurred in the physical and temporal world, temporary restorations of balance may occur, but they are overshadowed by the eventual return of imbalance. Only a restoration of balance that occurs beyond the physical world can restore a permanence of balance. Such a restoration, then, can only occur at the hands of Christ through His salvific work. As a means of shorthand, I will call this the Restoration Principle.

The Restoration Principle fleshes out the glories of God's self-revelation in the so-called "Book of Nature." Psalm 19:1–4 is foundational to this: "The heavens declare the glory of God, and the sky proclaims the work of His hands. Day after day they pour out speech; night after night they communicate knowledge. There is no speech; there are no words; their voice is not heard. Their message has gone out to all the earth, and their words to the ends of the world." The universe itself declares not only the presence of God but also His particular glories. This is no passive revelation: it is powerful, wordless speech that goes out to the entirety of earth and its peoples. Psalm 50:6 continues this active declaration, since "the heavens proclaim His righteousness, for God is the judge"; Ps 97:6 reiterates this proposition. Psalm 89:2,5 proposes that God's "faithfulness" is present in the heavens.

Paul is even more specific in Rom 1:16–20, tying nature's declarations of God's righteousness specifically to His Laws:

> For I am not ashamed of the gospel, because it is God's power for salvation to everyone who believes, first to the Jew, and also to the Greek. For in it God's righteousness is revealed from faith to faith, just as it is written: The righteous will live by faith. For God's wrath is revealed from heaven against all godlessness and unrighteousness of people who by their unrighteousness suppress the truth, since what can be known about God is evident among them, because God has shown it to them. For His invisible attributes, that is, His eternal power and divine nature, have been clearly seen since the creation of the world, being understood through what He has made. As a result, people are without excuse.

These invisible attributes are a part of God's Story, which He has written on the very hearts of humankind: "So, when Gentiles, who do not have the law, instinctively do what the law demands, they are a law to themselves even though they do not have the law. They show that the work of the law is written on their hearts. Their consciences confirm this. Their competing thoughts either accuse or excuse them on the day when God judges what people have kept secret, according to my gospel through Christ Jesus" (Rom 2:14–16).

These passages imply that the Restoration Principle must reflect God's works, righteousness, faithfulness, and law all in ways that are powerfully effective. Again, the presence of these elements is active enough that the heavens "declare" and "reveal" them. In fact, we can see these elements in the principles of balance, imbalance, and restoration. General revelation foreshadows the specifics of special revelation. The beauty and sheer power of the created world indicate a power that lies beyond the natural world. The justice of general revelation reveals the law and the sense of right and wrong with which God has charged all of creation. The loving-kindness that may be found in nature anticipates the specific sacrificial love that will be exemplified by Christ.

This, then, is not a squishy general revelation that is on the order of a cosmic Ziggy cartoon. This is a robust general revelation that employs the physical universe in ways that point to specific elements of God's nature: creativity, faithfulness, righteousness, and grace itself. Romans 1:20 ("His eternal power and divine nature, [which] have been clearly seen, being understood through what He has made. As a result, people are without excuse") adds a new element to Psalm 19's more general declaration of God's general revelation. We must be confronted with a realization that this is no benign declaration; the stakes of God's Story, of the Restoration Principle, are the highest possible. The created world does not simply point toward a general deity; it points toward a specific view of grace that comports with what I have called God's biblical story of balance, imbalance, and restoration.

A Universe Dripping with Grace: The Echoes of God's Story

In C. S. Lewis's description of the creation of Narnia in *The Magician's Nephew*, the narrator describes Aslan as singing the world into creation. As the song wafts through the world, it drops life throughout the fecund new world, echoing the song itself in the living things that arise from its notes: "The Lion was pacing to and fro about that empty land and singing his new song. It was softer and more lilting than the song by which he had called up the stars and the sun; a gentle, rippling music. And as he walked and sang the valley grew green with grass. It spread out from the Lion like a pool. It ran up the sides of the little hills like a wave."[6]

Lewis's imaginative retelling of the world's beginning is what we would expect from an artist: God as Singer, whose song resonates with the rest of His creation. The creation reflects His tender loving-kindness. It reflects His love of order and predictability, moderated with a dose of whimsy and joy. For Lewis, the world of Narnia itself bears testimony to the nature and character of its creator, even as it bears testimony to Lewis's Creator as well. In such a concept, Lewis is replicating the Christian doctrine of general revelation, the belief that God has revealed Himself to His creation through the world itself.

If, as the Scriptures plainly teach, the universe declares God's glory, then it also should point to His story at every turn. We should find the Restoration Principle present in many places that transcend both time and culture in ways that declare God's identity and purpose. We should find evidence that may be construed as pointing not just generally to a vague deity but rather to a specific deity, the God of the Bible, and to the need for redemption through His act of restoration. God's genius at making Himself manifest to His creation should cause all of creation to drip with His love toward us.

Recently, a number of works have appeared that outline the so-called "anthropic principle," the observation that the Earth seems to be situated uniquely in the universe to support human life. The most prominent of these is Guillermo Gonzalez and Jay W. Richards's *The Privileged Planet: How Our Place in the Cosmos Is Designed for Discovery*.[7] The anthropic principle draws on a number of evidences from the physical world, especially from astronomy, to indicate that God's loving-kindness toward us

---

[6] C. S. Lewis, *The Magician's Nephew* (London: Grafton, 1955), 97.
[7] G. Gonzalez and J. W. Richards, *The Privileged Planet: How Our Place in the Cosmos Is Designed for Discovery* (Washington, DC: Regnery, 2004).

began with the way that the universe itself was designed as a part of creation.

When I hold the Restoration Principle up to the created world, I see it in various forms almost everywhere, in settings that are both specifically natural and in others that are intrinsically human.

In the natural world, I note that the Restoration Principle roughly approximates the foundational concept of *equilibrium*. In equilibrium, balance of some sort is established (called the "stationary point") and is the default status of the system. If the balance is lost, then a closed system seeks to restore that balance. This principle appears throughout the universe.[8] Balance is sought, for imbalance creates tension that drives attempts toward restoration. Restoration in natural systems, however, is always fragile or tentative and may be lost.[9] This drive toward stasis or balance is reflected in many of the most basic laws of science, such as that of inertia (part of Newton's First Law of Motion, the tendency of bodies at rest or in motion to remain in that state until force or friction acts upon them) and the laws of thermodynamics (the natural tendency of systems to seek after the lowest possible balance of energy).

---

[8] The appearance of principles that point to God should not surprise us, even within the context of a scientific understanding of the world. As James Sire once noted, "Science itself was born from the Christian worldview that held that the universe is orderly because an omniscient and omnipotent God intended to make a world that reflected his own intelligence. The universe is orderly because God is Logos (intelligence itself)." J. W. Sire, *Naming the Elephant: Worldview as a Concept* (Downers Grove: IVP, 2004), 157

[9] This is a critical distinction between the Restoration Principle in the natural world and how it might be applied spiritually: in the created world, which is temporal and temporary, the Restoration Principle is constantly recycled in every way, as equilibrium is lost over and over, until the created world comes to its conclusion and a new heaven and a new earth are created, at which time Christ will have reconciled all things to Himself, ushering in an era in which, presumably, even the laws of nature will no longer reflect the creation-fall-redemption paradigm. Because salvation, the ultimate application of the Restoration Principle, is spiritual and therefore transcends the physical world, that mode of Restoration need not be fragile or repeated; this is an application of the theological concept of the "perseverance of the saints," wherein salvation is sealed at the moment of salvation.

Equilibrium / balance drives a number of diverse natural processes:

* *Plate Tectonics*: One of the unifying theories of geology is that of plate tectonics, the idea that the Earth's crust is covered with independent plates (part of the lithosphere) that float on the semiliquid portion of the crust called the asthenosphere. As these plates move, they create stress or friction against one another, pressing harder and increasing the pressure at fault lines (sometimes called rifts). The balance of the independent plates, then, falls into imbalance as the seismological pressure builds, until the pressure is too great and an earthquake occurs, bleeding the pressure and restoring, however temporarily, the balance between the plates.

* *Pressure Systems*: A well-worn bon mot attributed to Aristotle is that nature abhors a vacuum; emptiness in the created world always seeks after fullness. The ramifications of this principle are manifold. This explains how pumps work: the balance a closed system maintains is lost when the system is opened (through loss of pressure or through the addition of pressure), and the change in pressure (whether fluid or gas) forces the matter within the system to seek after the lower pressure level of the new system. This occurs because matter always seeks after the lowest level of energy possible, and a vacuum (or any state that is of a lower level of energy), always creates an imbalance of energy that seeks after a lower even as gas pressure constantly seeks to move to a lower level of energy. These principles affect meteorology, as air pressure systems move across the face of the earth. Most of us are familiar with how cold fronts affect the likelihood of severe weather: when a warm, moist air mass collides with a cool air mass, the friction between the two masses and the lack of equilibrium between the two systems creates

often violent weather, including massive thunderstorms and tornados.

* *Hydrological Cycle*: Water takes on three forms: liquid, gas (vapor), and solid (ice) in nature. Each form tends to remain stable until heat (which is affected by pressure forces as well) is introduced or removed. The balance present in ice is lost when heat is introduced; liquid water is produced. When the heat is removed, ice will reappear. With liquid water, when additional heat is applied, the water turns into a gaseous form. To some extent, it may be said that because of the earth's normal range of surface temperatures, the liquid form is the "default" state, in that vapor seems driven to return to liquid, even as ice tends to be restored to a liquid form.

* *Homeostasis*: In living creatures, the physical structures of a creature are contained in what is called a "closed system." The closed system allows the regulation of materials such as water or, in endothermic creatures, body heat, within the organism's body. Certain levels of materials are the default "norms," which the body seeks to maintain. When the body has too much water, for example, the systems perceive the imbalance and seek to restore the proper balance. When the body has too much heat, various systems perceive this and work to restore the proper temperature. Many familiar diseases are the result of homeostatic imbalances: diabetes, hypoglycemia, and gout. Well-functioning bodies always strive toward balance, and the restoration of that balance is critical to survival.

The Restoration Principle is not limited to the physical world, however. It appears in uniquely human areas as well, where our perceptions of the natural world are involved:

* *Musical Harmony*: In Western music, which builds on classical Greek musical theories, there is a specific, regu-

lar, and predictable structure to chords and their progressions. The word "harmony" itself is an Anglicized form of the Greek for "concordance" or "agreement," which explains the philosophy behind the theory. The goal is a pleasing sound that resolves or completes itself. A harmonic chord begins with a basic note, called the root, and then includes harmonic tones (based on the physics of the waveforms produced by musical instruments), most commonly the "third" and "fifth" in major chords, which were based on the so-called Pythagorian tuning law's principles (the traditional twelve-tone tuning scale). The harmonic tones amplify the root tone to create a fullness of tone that approximates a sense of aural perfection.[10] This philosophical approach to music and its mathematical foundations was applied even on grand scales, producing such concepts as the "music of the spheres," the supposed universal harmony of the planets themselves in their orbits. Modern and non-Western music theories often react against the notion of mathematical perfection, using dissonant chords or alternative tunings to create "interest" or other reactions to the compositions.[11] Nonetheless, the deeply seated response that we feel toward musical harmony is felt every time we hear a poorly tuned instrument or a poorly fingered chord. The loss of harmonic balance moves us deeply to crave a restoration of the balance.

    *   *Artistic Principles of Design*: At its most basic level, "art" means "arranged," which is to say that the artist arranges

---

[10] The perfection of a tripartite harmonic chord also serves as a helpful metaphor for the Holy Trinity, as each tone may be recognized on its own as a note, even as it is constantly and simultaneously a part of the totality of the overall chord itself.

[11] Avant-garde composer Frank Zappa has compared harmonically consistent compositions to eating "cottage cheese" or "watching a movie with only good guys in it" (quoted in Frank Zappa and Peter Occhiogrosso, *The Real Frank Zappa Book* [New York: Touchstone, 1989], n.p.; http://en.wikiquote.org/wiki/Frank_Zappa; (accessed on May 2, 2009). Zappa's point makes my case: disharmony creates in the listener a longing for resolution, a return to harmonic consistency or resolution.

a medium in such a way as to communicate an aesthetic message. In the visual arts, this means arranging 2- or 3-dimensional materials such as ink, chalk, or sculpted material into ways that approximate an object or a concept. Traditional art is governed by the principles of design, of which the first element is balance (the others are proportion, rhythm, emphasis, and unity). Balance in design dictates the composition of visual artworks, where a point or a plane in the work provides a fulcrum around which the work's elements appear. In traditional art, the goal is a balanced field of vision; contemporary art often reacts against this, creating a tension within the work's perception by the viewer through the intentional undermining of the balance, which causes the viewer to react in a subconscious way to the lack of balance. In artwork that seeks to create purely emotional responses, this seems to heighten the gut-level response through the use of affected anxiety. Anyone who has taken a photograph that is poorly shot (heads cut off, all of subjects on one side of shot and rest of shot empty, etc.) has experienced this sense of frustration over anxiety. The same applies when we walk into a room that contains framed art and the frames are askew. Most of us can barely suppress the desire to straighten the frame back into alignment with traditional perpendiculars, restoring the lost balance.

I readily admit that I am, perhaps, oversimplifying these principles, but the general principles seem to match up in ways that are fascinating. The more I study the various understandings of our world, the more commonly I see the Restoration Principle at work.

These kinds of natural world applications of the Restoration Principle can also aid us in the interpretation of biblical revelation. Homeostasis, for example, actually appears in biblical revelation. One of the ways that homeostasis functions is in water regulation. Water is necessary for proper metabolic function. In plants we call an imbalance of water "being parched"; most of us have seen a houseplant that has dried out, hanging limply in its pot, only to perk up when it is watered generously. A plant that is not watered, however, becomes dehydrated. In both plants and animals, dehydration can lead to cell death or systemic failure.

In animals, we call the water imbalance "thirst." Psalm 42:1–2 declares, "As a deer longs for streams of water, so I long for You, God. I thirst for God, the living God. When can I come and appear before God?" This image is popular as a hymn lyric and as a prayer, but the full effects of the metaphor are not completely understood apart from examining it from the perspective of homeostasis, as understood through the Restoration Principle. This passage is, in fact, a declaration that the biological processes that govern life in all animals *themselves* point to the need that we all have for restoration in and through God.

All organisms have a complex system of control over their internal water levels, starting from single-celled organisms (which use permeable membranes to pass water molecules back and forth) to plants (which use the stoma cell complexes in their leaves to regulate internal water levels) to the thirst reflex in higher order animals (which triggers specific cravings to consume water, a way to offset the loss of water through respiration or perspiration). When the deer longs for water, it is because its body has moved from balance to imbalance; the imbalance has created a specific need that cannot be satisfied through any other means. Water, and water alone, can slake the thirst.

In the same way, our fallen nature has thrown our souls off balance and has generated a deep longing inside us that craves after the kind of satisfaction that only God's grace can afford. As the psalmist says, we thirst for the living God, to find ourselves standing in His presence as restored creatures whose fallen spiritual state has been satisfied through His redemption. The image of the deer is not simply an image of thirst, for it is an affirmation that the way that God designed the very physics of the universe, laws that create the sense of thirst in a deer, reflect the gospel itself: we all have a longing that can only be satisfied in God Himself. We may intuit this longing based on our need for water, food, salt, or almost any other essential of life.

This biblical metaphor of thirst occurs in Psalm 23 as well (the "still waters" being, among other things, for drinking), Ps 63:1 ("I thirst for You"), Ps 107:9 ("For He has satisfied the thirsty"), and many other places, but it is picked back up in the New Testament as well, particularly in John 4, when Christ encounters the woman at the well. When he asks for a drink of water from the woman (v. 7), her response causes Him to explain the connection between literal water and the eternal Water of His salvation: "Everyone who drinks from this water will get thirsty again. But whoever drinks from the water that I will give him will never get thirsty again—ever! In fact, the water I will give him will become a well of water springing up within him for eternal life" (vv. 13–14). The natural water is trapped in an endless cycle of homeostatic balance, imbalance, and restoration because it is a function of the principles of this world, but Christ proposes that the eternal water will break that cycle, providing perpetual satisfaction and restoration that will transcend anything we will ever know in this world.[12] When Christ talks about the creatures of this world finding their needs being taken care of in God, it is more than just a statement of providence; it is also a statement about the nature of God's ultimate care. It is not found in this world but rather in *Him*.

A homeostatic reading even provides a fresh understanding of Prov 25:21: "If your enemy is hungry, give him food to eat, and if he is thirsty, give him water to drink." This passage is not simply about being kind to enemies in order to heap coals on their heads; it is about bringing a foreshadowing of the Gospel itself to our enemies in order to effect an eternal change in them. The same applies to Christ's admonition in Matt 25:31–46 to care for "the

---

[12] Note that the consistency of biblical imagery throughout the Scriptures and the linkage of such images as "hunger" and "thirst" and their correlative terms "eat" and "drink" into the very heart of Christian practice through both communion and service to poor persons implies that biblical imagery is not mere ornamentation to the language of the Bible. Such images bridge the gap between general revelation and special revelation, harnessing God's revelation of Himself in ways that allow us to comprehend His redemptive mission in our world.

least of these" by providing food, water, and clothing. Providing the basics of life foreshadows providing the basics of eternity.

Finally, I cannot write of balance without further calling to mind the Oriental cultural emphasis on balance and harmony, often called the Tao. In this conception, the universe is governed by a universal force that expresses itself in a sort of natural, default mode within the physical world, a kind of harmony of being. While I cannot illuminate here the various intricacies of *Tao Te Ching* and its followers, I can note that the concept of balance-imbalance-restoration is not simply foundational to Western thought; its principle dominates Eastern culture.[13] Most Westerners will recognize the yin-yang symbol, the basic icon of Taoism, which represents the ultimate balance and harmony of the universe. Taoism celebrates rest and peace, qualities that the Judeo-Christian tradition celebrates as a part of the goal of shalom, or divine peace that God imbues in the universe. Taoism also celebrates a kind of moral law that finds its clearest expression in social and psychological harmony.

C. S. Lewis celebrates a generalized version of the Tao in *The Abolition of Man*, where he espouses its application as natural law.[14] In his detailed exploration of the concept, he discusses Tao as more of a moral principle than a unifying principle of the

---

[13] Perhaps few metaphysical concepts have influenced contemporary sciences more than the concept of the integration of the principles of the Tao and scientific theory. In 1975, Frijtof Capra capitalized on this connection in his bestselling *The Tao of Physics: An Exploration of the Parallels between Modern Physics and Eastern Mysticism,* 4th ed. (Boston: Shambhala, 2000); Gary Zukav's *The Dancing Wu Li Masters: An Overview of the New Physics* (New York: Harper-One, 2001) further developed some of these concepts and moved into the realm of popular culture through Oprah Winfrey's later promotion of his books. I might add that as an undergraduate science student in a state university in the early 1980s, I found that the only overlap between science and metaphysics that was deemed as allowable was in works like these. The only time I ever heard religious faith discussed in a positive light was by a physics professor who had converted to Buddhism based on his connection between Taoist principles and the advent of quantum physics.

[14] Again, see C. S. Lewis's discussions of the Tao within a Christian context in *The Abolition of Man* (New York: HarperSanFrancisco, 1974). For Lewis, the Tao reflects God's natural law as expressed through general revelation.

created world. I have found it profitable to extend Lewis's thinking into the realm of natural, and not simply moral, principles.

In all of these processes, then, we see God's story in ways that reflect the very nature of the gospel: in balance, we intuit the perfection of things that are created by God, even as we realize that perfection in this world cannot last. In imbalance, we find rationality to the chaos and disharmony that fills this world, including our own lives and relationships. In our states of imbalance, we hunger to regain the balance that we have seen as peaceful and for which we all long. When a cold front approaches and we know that the atmosphere is charged with energy, each of us longs for the front to pass quickly, so that we can experience the relief that comes when the energy in the air is restored to a state of lower energy. This is a lesser reflection of the same sense that we have when we realize that our sins have disrupted a harmony in our lives that must somehow be restored.

The world itself groans for the coming of Christ. It is filled with longings and cravings, from the very elements of the world to the systems that dominate living organisms, which cannot be ended until Christ Himself returns to usher in a new heavens and a new earth, where His presence will transcend the old needs and brokenness. As John the Divine said, "He will wipe away every tear from their eyes. Death will exist no longer; grief, crying, and pain will exist no longer, because the previous things have passed away" (Rev 21:4). Eternity is not simply balance restored for all of eternity: it is balance supplanted with God's eternal, loving presence.

The Restoration Principle Applied

Over the years, I have heard many "preachers' stories" about how general revelation can play a role in someone's ultimate conversion to Christianity, but when I studied medieval literature in English courses, I read such a story from English history.

The Venerable Bede (c. 673–735) records the story of King Edwin of Northumberland at the hands of the missionary bishop Paulinus. Edwin was willing to hear the preaching of Paulinus and to convert at once, but he called together a meeting of his council of elders, which included his pagan high priest, Coifi. Paulinus presented the gospel to him, and one of the chief advisors replied with this observation:

> Your Majesty, when we compare the present life of man on earth with that time of which we have no knowledge, it seems to me like the swift flight of a single sparrow through the banqueting-hall where you are sitting at dinner on a winter's day with your thegns and counsellors. In the midst there is a comforting fire to warm the hall; outside, the storms of winter rain or snow are raging. This sparrow flies swiftly in through one door of the hall, and out through another. While he is inside, he is safe from the winter storms; but after a few moments of comfort, he vanishes from sight into the wintry world from which he came. Even so, man appears on earth for a little while; but of what went before this life or of what follows, we know nothing. Therefore, if this new teaching has brought any more certain knowledge, it seems only right that we should follow it.[15]

The advisor was stating the insight that something he had observed in nature had created in him an imbalance, a longing for something more. Clearly drawn on a personal experience of watching such a sparrow's flight, the advisor heard the gospel of redemption and eternal life as the restoration of that balance that had been lost.

Moreover, Coifi, the chief priest, revealed that he too had found in his own observations of life and nature an imbalance:

> I have long realized that there is nothing in our way of worship; for the more diligently I thought [sic] after truth in our religion, the less I found.

[15] Bede, *Ecclesiastical History of the English People*, rev. ed., trans. L. Sherley-Price (New York: Penguin, 1968), 129–30.

> I now publicly confess that this teaching clearly
> reveals truths that will afford us the blessings of
> life, salvation, and eternal happiness. Therefore,
> Your Majesty, I submit that the temples and altars
> that we have dedicated to no advantage be imme-
> diately desecrated and burned.[16]

Immediately, the council sets out, and Coifi destroys the very pagan worship centers that he himself had dedicated. These men's minds had been unsettled by the imbalance of perspective and sense of truth that they saw in their day-to-day lives, and had been spurred to recognize God's special revelation when they finally heard it.

In my own family, a similar story was central to my grandfather's life. In his final years, Grandfather, Thomas Edison Fant, told me many stories about his young adulthood. He had been a businessman, a pastor, and a dog trainer through six decades of work and had led a very interesting life. He repeated one story many times, what he called his "pre-conversion" experience of faith.

Abandoned by his parents at a very early age, Grandfather reared himself, renting a room and holding several jobs to support himself. He was less than ten years old when this began, trying to balance going to school, working those jobs, and dealing with his grief over being left behind.

The loneliness, he said, was the hardest part. He had no time for friends or play since he worked all the time and usually slept only four or five hours between his evening and morning jobs. He had no mother's care when he was sick. He had no father's approval when he did well. He watched other families and wondered what was wrong with him that had caused his parents to reject him.

After a couple of years, he had reached his limit. He decided to kill himself, figuring that no one would miss him. That evening, he cleaned his rifle and found a sturdy stick that he could place

---

[16] Bede, *Ecclesiastical History,* 130.

against his trigger to press with his feet. He would need to use his feet because his arms were too short to reach the trigger with the barrel in his mouth. He wrote a brief will, leaving his scant belongings to the persons whom he felt had helped him survive even that long.

At midnight, he entered the Gum Log Cemetery and found a freshly dug grave (he did not want to bother anyone with having to dig a grave for him). He sat on a nearby headstone and gathered his courage. He placed the stout stick in the trigger box and put the barrel of the gun in his mouth. As he prepared to put his feet on the stick, he took one last look at the sky. It was a particularly cold night, and the stars were incredibly vivid.

He was startled, he recounted, by the beauty of the stars, even though he had seen them every night of his life. He took the barrel of the gun out of his mouth in order to turn his head in different directions, taking in all of the constellations. In that moment, he was overcome with a single thought: *If there is a God who made such beauty, then maybe He might love even a little boy like me whom no one else wants.* For some reason, this thought comforted and strengthened him. What if there were a God who could transcend circumstances and reach beyond pain?

Grandfather had almost never been to church in his life, and he did not go to church even then. He left the cemetery and went on with his life, becoming a successful businessman until he was in his thirties, when he attended an evangelistic crusade and had what he called his "real" conversion experience. As he began to study his Bible, he was astonished the first time he read Ps 97:6: "The heavens proclaim His righteousness; all the peoples see His glory." In that passage, he saw clearly the thought that had seized his mind. He was not converted in that moment, he did not know of Christ's grace yet, but he did sense that God was righteous and loving. For the first time in his life, he had discovered hope.

Through the work of the Holy Spirit, general revelation points toward special revelation, which points toward the incarnation. The Restoration Principle points toward redemption, which has been made possible by Christ's work of grace. Christ's earthly ministry generated echoes that may be seen throughout the world.

What about human narrative? If the Restoration Principle works in so many other areas, including the musical and visual arts, then surely it works as the framework for narrative art as well. Indeed, I see this framework everywhere I look in literature as well. In God's Story, I also see a foundation for a fresh understanding of human stories. In order to see it, however, I would perhaps be well-served to delve into historical understandings of narrative before applying the Restoration Principle. I am, however, overwhelmed by the Principle's persistence throughout the broad span of human storytelling, for within the Restoration Principle I see a Restoration Narrative that echoes throughout human cultures. Before I can apply the Restoration Narrative to other stories, however, I need to examine some of the ways that literary critics have analyzed stories throughout history. In these hermeneutical strategies, I hope we can begin to see how the Restoration Narrative might function through a reading of narrative as understood in the light of general revelation and God's Story.

4

Finding God's Story in Narrative Structure

> They show that the work of the law is written on their hearts. Their consciences confirm this.
>
> —Rom 2:15

> The truth is clear:
> Almighty God rules over mankind and always has.
>
> Beowulf (trans. Seamus Heaney)
> lines 700-702

One of my junior high school teachers gave us a bit of independence by allowing us to determine our own grade through a contract syllabus. For each nine-week unit, we could earn an A by reading ten books and writing reports on them; for a B, we had to handle eight books, and so forth, down to a minimum threshold of four books for a D. We selected our target grade and completed the assignments on our own timetable.

Oddly enough, I only remember one of the books I wrote about: the original novel *Star Wars*, by George Lucas, which predated the 1977 film. I bought it off the rack in a drug store before making a bus trip to see my grandparents in Mississippi. I dutifully wrote out my report, detailing how young Luke Skywalker left a fairly quiet life on Tatooine and became a Jedi apprentice under the tutelage of Obi Wan Kenobi, fought against the evil Darth Vader, and just when everything seemed the darkest, was able to destroy the Death Star by using the special powers endowed by The Force. I then concluded with a paragraph explaining why I liked the book so much.

In hindsight, I know that what I was producing was an old-fashioned plot summary, starting at the beginning and moving to the conclusion, with a brief critique tacked on for good measure. I did not really analyze the book's prose or the thematic elements at all.

The basic plot outline employed by most writers, with a beginning, a middle, and an end, reflects the persistent framework that transcends both time and culture. The idea that stories have a beginning, a middle, and an end sounds ridiculously simplistic, but it is basic to almost all storytelling. Some stories follow this structure chronologically, some mix past and present and future into different phrasings, but pretty much all of them start, move to some sort of conflict, and then conclude in a way that is consistent with the rest of the story's action. More recent literature, especially postmodern fiction, tries to rebel against this framework, but in some ways the very fact that it rebels against it reveals the true persistence of the progression.

Literary critics have analyzed the structures and dominant themes of narrative for millennia. Through traditional methods like formalism, they have tried to link form with meaning. Through nontraditional methods like deconstructionism, they have tried to disconnect form from meaning, while perhaps actually underscoring the importance of structuralism in the interpretive process.[1] Literary criticism and hermeneutics are themselves a part of an overarching story of how humankind has approached narrative. In the West, a number of important critical tools have long dominated the reading and interpretation of narrative texts.

Aristotelian Poetics

If all of Western philosophy is but a footnote to Plato (c. 427–327 BC), as Alfred North Whitehead famously declared, then all of Western literary criticism began as a footnote to Aristotle. Plato was not a fan of literary production (in fact, he banned poets from his republic![2]), and he termed any kind of art as ultimately a failure because of his Theory of Ideas. As T. S. Dorsch explains, "According to this theory everything that exists, or happens, in this world is an imperfect copy of an ideal object or action or state that has an ideal existence beyond this world. The productions of the poets (and artists) are therefore imitations of imperfect copies of an ideal life; they are third-hand and unreal, and can teach us nothing of value about life."[3] This means, then, that any art that imitates life is a copy of a copy, and poets are promulgators of defective views of the ultimate reality.

Before Plato, Socrates (c. 469–399 BC) had likewise castigated poets as defective in their work. As Dorsch notes, Socrates argued that "God is perfectly good, and therefore both changeless and incapable of deceit, but the poets often show him as falling

---

[1] What I mean here is that when poststructuralist criticism says that writing is wholly ineffective in communicating transcendent meaning, it commits the worst kind of logical fallacy, as their comments themselves are written in a mode of discourse (the critical essay) that itself uses a specific structure to communicate meaning.

[2] See T. S. Dorsch, "Introduction," *Classical Literary Criticism* (New York: Penguin, 1965), 10.

[3] Dorsch, "Introduction," 12.

short in these respects; they misrepresent gods and heroes, 'like a portrait painter who fails to catch a likeness', and thus in the theological sense they are unsuitable preceptors."[4]

Aristotle (384–322 BC) sought to rescue art from such a viewpoint, and in his landmark *Ars Poetica*, he outlined how the poet, in particular, could transform our vision of life through a new kind of idealism, the notion that art could elevate our sensibilities. All artists have this capacity, and a poet, whose medium is language, seeks after "the representation of life; necessarily, therefore, he must always represent things in one of three ways: either as they were or are, or as they are said to be or seem to be, or as they ought to be."[5] This is why he viewed poetics as an ethical pursuit, especially in tragedy, where the dramatist sought to stir the audience's pity through "undeserved misfortune, and our fear by that of someone just like ourselves—pity for the undeserving sufferer and fear for the man like ourselves—so that the situation in question would have nothing in it either pitiful or fearful. . . . The change in fortune will be, not from misery to prosperity, but the reverse, from prosperity to misery, and it will be due, not to depravity, but to some great error."[6] Thus, using drama and epic poetry as his primary exempla, Aristotle created a systemic analysis of how poetic treatments could communicate truth to audiences.

Aristotle noted that narratives consistently included three parts—a beginning, a middle, and an end—that provided a structure for relating the story's plot elements. The terms for these parts relate to the story's structure, not to its plot. In classical forms, the story generally begins *in medias res* ("in the midst of things"), with the plot's beginning related in the *prostasis* as the story unfolds. For tragedy, that starting point leads immediately to the story's complication, which "consists of the incidents lying outside the plot, and often some of those inside it, and the rest is the denouement. By complication I mean the part of the story from

---

[4] Dorsch, "Introduction," 11.
[5] Aristotle, "On the Art of Poetry," in *Classical Literary Criticism,* trans. T. S. Dorsch (New York: Penguin, 1965), 69.
[6] Aristotle, "On the Art of Poetry," 48.

the beginning to the point immediately preceding the change to good or bad fortune; by denouement the part from the onset of this change to the end."[7] In tragedy, the complications result from the hero's tragic flaw, generally called the *hamartia*.[8] The turning point between complication and denouement is the story's climax, the moment when the conflict reaches its height.

Classical dramatic structure was built around conflicts that gave rise to the ultimate climax of the play. The process was akin to that of knot-tying. As William Harmon and Hugh Holman have noted,

> The ancients compared the plot of a drama to the tying and untying of a knot. The principle of dramatic conflict, though not mentioned as such in Aristotle's definition of drama, is implied in this figure. The technical structure of a serious play is determined by the necessities of developing this dramatic conflict. Thus, a well-built tragedy will commonly show the following divisions, each representing a phase of the dramatic conflict: introduction, rising action, climax or crisis (turning point), falling action, and catastrophe.... This structure based on the analogy of the tying and untying of a knot is applicable to comedy, the novel, and the short story, with the adjustment of the use of the broader term *dénouement* for catastrophe in works that are not tragic.[9]

Perhaps the best known classical play is Sophocles' *Oedipus Rex* (c. 335 BC), which also provided Aristotle much of his material.[10] That story opens with Oedipus already seated as the king of

---

[7] Aristotle, "On the Art of Poetry," 56.
[8] Bible scholars will recognize *hamartia* as a biblical term as well: it is the term used in the Greek New Testament for "sin."
[9] William Harmon and Hugh Holman, "Dramatic structure," *A Handbook to Literature,* 10th ed. (Upper Saddle River: Pearson Prentice Hall, 2006), 171–172.
[10] Sophocles, *Oedipus the King (Oedipus Rex),* in *Norton Anthology of World Literature,* vol. A, 2nd ed., trans. R. Fagles (New York: W. W. Norton, 2002).

Thebes, ruling alongside his wife Jocasta and her brother Creon. The city is in the midst of a terrible plague that has killed scores of its citizens. The dialogue provides the audience with background information about Oedipus's life, as well as that of Jocasta and her late husband Laertes. The audience knows of the irony of their relationship, which in turn produces a sharp irony that undergirds much of the characters' words. The conflict finally reaches a peak, climaxing as Oedipus realizes the truth in horror, and the play moves toward its conclusion with Jocasta's suicide and Oedipus's self-inflicted blindness and exile.

Oedipus moves effortlessly through Aristotle's structural outlines, carrying the audience from horror to pity as Sophocles declares the foolishness of challenging the wisdom of the gods. In the process, the audience is reminded that they themselves are prone to similar foolishness, experiencing the communal catharsis ("cleansing") of emotions that make classical tragedy so powerful. Few writers have shared Sophocles' ability to create conflict that crushes the audience with empathy.

Aristotle sought to describe how classical drama functioned structurally, but in his wake, his descriptions became prescriptions, setting the standards that would be followed by millennia of storytellers. For generations, producers of narrative, whether dramatic or not, have borrowed from Aristotle and other classical thinkers, moving the whole of storytelling into modes that focus on conflict. While the pattern was already present, Aristotle codified it, in the West at least, in ways that continue to structure our storytelling.

Freytag's Triangle

Gustav Freytag (1816–1895) produced his landmark work of criticism, *Die Technik des Drama* (1863), as an exploration of the structural workings of drama, picking up where Aristotle had left off. Whereas Aristotle had generated an entire philosophy of poetics based on classical drama, Freytag focused on the structures of plot, analyzing how and why plot structures seem to function in the ways that they do. While Freytag originally applied his work to classical drama, his structural elements have been applied more broadly to most traditional narrative. As literary critics James S. Brown and Scott D. Yarbrough stated quite boldly: "[E]very narrative also has a structure. . . . One of the most convenient ways of discussing plot is through consideration of Freytag's pyramid."[11] Their comment reflects just how basic Freytag's pyramid (also called Freytag's triangle) has become as a foundational descriptor in the discussion of narrative; different versions of the graph form of the pyramid are included in many introductory texts on literary criticism.

Harmon and Holman link classical dramatic structure to a latter generation discussion found in Freytag, who had picked back up on the image of the tying and untying of a knot: "The relation of these [dramatic] parts is sometimes represented graphically by the figure of a pyramid, called Freytag's Pyramid, the rising slope suggesting the rising action or tying of the knot, the falling slope the falling action or resolution, the apex representing the climax."[12] Freytag's basic parts of dramatic action revolve around the conflict that the story conveys.

In the opening, we have the exposition, which provides the information necessary to understand the story. Audiences require information about characters, setting, and relationships in order to make sense of the conflict that will occur, information that allows them to have a stake in the action themselves. From the exposition, the story moves to inciting a moment that produces the rising action. The rising action draws the audience into a further emotional investment in the story, connecting them with the plight of the characters. The rising action, when effective, is like a rip tide that sweeps the audience up into the story's movements.

The climax is the point at which the movements shift into their greatest power, from good to bad (in the case of tragedies) or from bad to good (in the case of comedies). The climax produces the greatest amount of empathy from the audience; it is the tipping

---

[11] J. S. Brown and S. D. Yarbrough, *A Practical Introduction to Literary Study* (Upper Saddle River, NJ: Pearson Prentice Hall, 2005), 51.
[12] Harmon and Holman, *A Handbook to Literature,* 171.

point where all of the action culminates in a moment of clarity for characters and the audience. The climax then begins to fall, the sense of action moving back toward a lesser sense of urgency. The falling action ushers the audience toward a sense of resolution, a sense that justice is served or loose ends are being rewoven.

The final moments, the denouement, resolve the crisis, returning the story to a sense of restored order, even if the order has resulted from disaster or utter ruin. The story's ending returns the narrative's energy to the lowest possible level, with a sense of peace or a "glimpse of restored order."[13]

Freytag takes Aristotelian theory and reiterates the action itself, focusing on the very human portions of the audience's emotional investment in the narrative. While Aristotle's approach to narrative was descriptive of the best works of his day, Freytag codified the critical weight of the subsequent centuries' treatment of Aristotelian poetics into a much more prescriptive brand of poetics. Almost immediately, Freytag's triangle became standard to our understanding of how narrative functions structurally. Even as post-structuralist theorists of the latter twentieth century react against Freytag, their reaction is a kind of affirmation of his work. Also, like Aristotle, Freytag has cast a long shadow over the production and analysis of literary narrative, as his observations have been taken as prescriptive for storytellers of all kinds.

The Journey of Experience

The undertaking of a journey is so basic to narrative that we hardly notice it. From the quests of King Arthur's Roundtable to the pilgrims of Chaucer's *Canterbury Tales* to Gilgamesh's journey to visit Utnapishtim or Huckleberry Finn's river trip, protagonists have been having adventures for millennia.

Journeys have long been understood as metaphorical parallels to our experiences of life itself. We leave our past behind as we travel into the future, gathering experiences along the way which alter our understanding of life and our place in it until our former selves, which were innocent in some way, are transformed by our

---

[13] Harmon and Holman, *A Handbook to Literature,* 172.

experiences into new selves, ones that have reached a point of resignation about our place in the universe, a sense of transcendence about the role experience plays in shaping our self-awareness, or even the completion that comes from returning home.

Journeys of experience are sometimes called pilgrimages (when a religious or other meditative purpose is involved), a quest (when a specific, unifying purpose is assigned), or an exile (when a punitive reason, whether just or not, is a part of the wandering). Sometimes the travel is global (Jules Verne's *Around the World in Eighty Days*), and sometimes it barely covers a few city blocks (James Joyce's "Araby"). Sometimes the journey is actually symbolic and never includes a literal trip (William Blake's complementary books of poetry: *Songs of Innocence* and *Songs of Experience*).

The journey is the setting, a symbolic means for effecting the changes in the protagonist. Typically, the hero begins in a place of comfort, often home, and something causes him to embark on a path that will lead him toward a new understanding of the world around him. The comforts of home are lost, as is the innocence that must be shed reptilelike along the way. The struggles and complications that occur on the journey pile up, each one producing an experience that chips away at the former naivety that begins to transform. At some point, a climax occurs, with the protagonist facing a realization that he must do something with this knowledge. He must choose to embrace the weariness that accompanies such acquired wisdom (in an eerie echo of Eccl 1:18), or to reject it (seeking after some kind of new utopia), or even to determine that the best strategy is to transcend the experience in ways that achieve peace. This moment is often called the epiphany, and it tips the point from conflict to resolution.

The *Bildungsroman*, a subgenre of the novel, is a specific exploration of the journey of experience, one that carries a young man (or woman) through these stages. While the *Bildungsroman* was specifically started in Germany in the nineteenth century (the term was coined by Johann Carl Simon Morganstern), it really describes a great number of these kinds of stories that predate the term and come after it. Other terms were formerly used (such as *Kunstlerroman*, *Erziehungsroman*, and *Entwicklungsroman*, which had very specific traits as kinds of journeys of experience that were related to authorship, education, and personal growth, respectively) but tend to be absorbed into the larger term. For some readers, *Bildungsroman* may carry a broad enough meaning that it can include almost all journeys of experience.

In each of these cases, the journey throws the protagonist's life out of balance and he is driven to find some sort of resolution to his situation. Experience is the fuel that drives both the imbalance and, often, the discovery of an acceptance about life that restores peace.

The Restoration Principle as Narrative

As I was researching the initial stages of this book, Donald Miller's *Blue Like Jazz* dominated my conversations with students. Many of them viewed Miller's frank expressions of faith and doubt as a refreshing kind of authenticity, a quality that is greatly prized by their generation.

Miller is an inveterate storyteller, and his fascination with story as a process informs the way that he understands faith as a whole. For example, he related an epiphany he had while taking a creative writing course that discussed the basic characteristics of narrative. As he pondered writing, he wrote, an "odd thought occurred to me while I was studying that we don't know where the elements of story come from. I mean, we might have a guy's name who thought of them, but we don't know why they exist. I started wondering why the heart and mind responded to this specific formula when it came to telling stories."[14] Aristotle, Freytag, and others may be the guys "who thought of them" (the elements of story), but Miller is correct that no one has ever explained why these elements are so persistent and heart-moving, much less why they exist at all.

---

[14] D. Miller, *Blue Like Jazz: Nonreligious Thoughts on Christian Spirituality* (Nashville: Thomas Nelson, 2003), 31.

As I myself studied Aristotle, Freytag, and the Journey of Experience over these decades, for some reason I never had noticed how well the three approaches end up aligning themselves with one another. Aristotle and Freytag overlap, of course, because of their source materials, but the journey from innocence to experience to resolution had never synced up in the same way until I applied the Restoration Narrative to other stories. Suddenly, I began to see that Freytag's pyramid might be expanded to include all three elements (see figure 4.1):

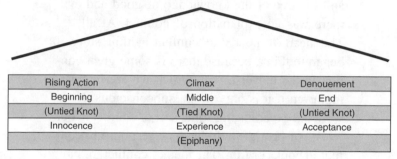

Rising Action	Climax	Denouement
Beginning	Middle	End
(Untied Knot)	(Tied Knot)	(Untied Knot)
Innocence	Experience	Acceptance
	(Epiphany)	

Figure 4.1: Linkage of Narrative Elements

These elements not only match up with one another; they seem to match the Restoration Narrative's elements of balance, imbalance, and restoration. If this is so, then it means that the basic structures of much of human narrative follow the basic gospel story elements of creation, fall, and redemption (see figure 4.2).

Creation	Fall	Redemption
Balance	Imbalance	Restoration
Rising Action	Climax	Denouement
Beginning	Middle	End
(Untied Knot)	(Tied Knot)	(Untied Knot)
Innocence	Experience	Acceptance
	(Epiphany)	

Figure 4.2: Linkage of Narrative Elements
with Restoration Narrative and Gospel Elements

Miller intuited this connection in *Blue Like Jazz*. As he explored the idea of conflict in narrative, he was struck by

> the idea of original sin and the birth of conflict. The rebellion against God explained why humans experienced conflict in their lives, and nobody knows or has any explanation other than this. . . . Without the Christian explanation of original sin, the seemingly silly story about Adam and Eve and the tree of the knowledge of good and evil, there was no explanation of conflict. At all. . . . The heart responds to conflict within story, I began to think, because there is some great conflict in the universe with which we are interacting, even if it is only in the subconscious. If we were not experiencing some sort of conflict in our lives, our hearts would have no response to conflict in books or film. The idea of conflict, of having tension, suspense, or an enemy, would make no sense to us. . . . As much as I did not want to admit it, Christian spirituality explained why.

> . . . Every good story has a climax. Climax is where a point of decision determines the end of the story. Now this was starting to scare me a little bit. If the human heart uses the tools of reality to create the elements of story, and the human heart responds to climax in the structure of story, this means that climax, or point of decision, could very well be something that exists in the universe. What I mean is that there is a decision the human heart needs to make. The elements of story began to parallel my understanding of Christian spirituality. Christianity offered a decision, a climax. It also offered a good and a bad resolution. In part,

  our decisions were instrumental to the way our
story turned out.[15]

Narrative, thus, may be viewed as finding its very essence, the root
of its structure, in God's overarching story of His own self-revelation. Various ways of understanding how we may interpret narrative, then, all combine under the meta-allegory of God's Story,
consistent with the divine meta-metaphor of God as Author.

  Such a convergence of narrative's basic structures along the
lines of the Restoration Narrative, however, also seems to invert
how we read these other structures. Instead of the classical notion
of tying and untying a knot, the knot is rather *untied* and *retied*.
Instead of the action rising and fall, the action instead *falls,* as one
might fall off a cliff and feel anxiety, and then rises as the climax
rebounds toward a resolution. Experience likewise creates anxiety
until the protagonist is able to find a way to make peace with his
new understandings of the world, which creates a kind of acceptance that produces at least some sense of stability in the world.
Perhaps the plot pyramid may be inverted along the lines of this
chart (see figure 4.3):

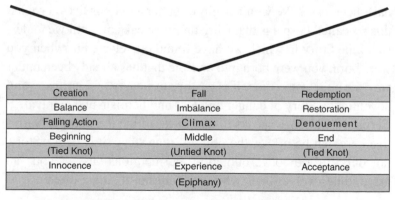

Creation	Fall	Redemption
Balance	Imbalance	Restoration
Falling Action	Climax	Denouement
Beginning	Middle	End
(Tied Knot)	(Untied Knot)	(Tied Knot)
Innocence	Experience	Acceptance
	(Epiphany)	

Figure 4.3: Narrative Elements Inverted

  All of this brings me back to Miller's original observation that
we do not know where the elements of narrative actually come
from. What if they derive specifically from God's self-revelation

---

[15] Miller, *Blue Like Jazz,* 32–33.

of Himself? What if they are a part of general revelation? This would explain why stories hold together the way that they do, as well as why they move us so deeply. If God has left us with a specific void inside of ourselves that craves its completion in Him, then we should long for resolution and restoration. We should be strangely moved by hints of it in various places. This proposition would mean that the biblical metaphor of God as Author is not simply an abstraction but rather is insightful in understanding narrative itself, with the Restoration Narrative serving as an interpretive key.

Like Miller, John Eldredge has intuited the linkage between narrative and God's revelation of Himself. Eldredge declared, "Christianity, in its true form, tells us that there is an Author and that he is good, the essence of all that is good and beautiful and true, for he is the source of all these things."[16] In this way, he affirmed the Author-Creator connection that is consistent with God's special revelation of Himself. Eldredge, however, went on to ask, "What if all the great stories that have ever moved you, brought you joy or tears—what if they are telling you something about the *true* Story into which you were born, the Epic into which you have been cast? We won't begin to understand our lives, or what this so-called gospel is that Christianity speaks of, until we understand the Story in which we have found ourselves. For when you were born, you were born into an Epic that has already been under way for quite some time. It is a Story of beauty and intimacy and adventure, a Story of danger and loss and heroism and betrayal."[17] Certainly, Eldredge speaks to the power of the Restoration Narrative here, but he misses the point of that Story: it is *God's* Story, not ours. In the above quotation, he mentions "us" / "you" an astounding twelve times while making not a single reference to

---

[16] J. Eldredge, *Epic: The Story God Is Telling and the Role That Is Yours to Play* (Nashville: Thomas Nelson, 2004), 14. Miller and Eldredge both eschew traditional systematic theology in favor of narrative theology. In this way, both are illustrative of the problem inherent in the second-generation narrative theologians who miss out on the full power of special revelation in Scripture. Their error is matched and inverted, however, by many systematic theologians, who miss out on the full power of narrative.

[17] Eldredge, *Epic,* 15.

God. The Restoration Narrative is not our story, for if it were, it would be weak, indeed, and quickly become irrelevant. Instead, it is God's timeless self-revelation, His reaching out across time and dimension to seek after the restoration of the broken relationship He has with His creation. He is the hermeneutical key; humanity is not.

The Restoration Narrative Applied to Biblical Narrative

Previously, I emphasized the idea that general revelation must be subject to the authority of special revelation. Because of this, I think that I must turn to biblical narrative to see if what I have proposed as the Restoration Narrative can be identified in the stories that the Bible contains, as evidence that the Narrative matches the Story of special revelation. If biblical narratives typically reflect the Restoration Narrative, then they would fit in with God's overarching Story.

Almost everywhere we turn in the Old Testament, we find stories that follow the framework of balance, imbalance, and restoration. Other stories do not follow the framework in its entirety in their Old Testament setting, but do find the longed for restoration ultimately in the New Testament (Adam and Eve's expulsion from the garden would be one example, as would also be the tower of Babel). More times than not, however, the narrative is followed, though the ultimate (and permanent) restoration of each story is found in the coming of Christ and, finally, in Christ's ministry of reconciliation of all things to Himself (Col 1:20).

In Noah, for example (Gen 6–9), the preponderance of sin that had run rampant throughout the human realm had thrown the world out of balance. In fact, the situation was made dire by the involvement of the "sons of God" (Gen 6:2). God instructed Noah to prepare for the coming flood and for God's direct intervention through the saving method of the ark. The story reached its climax as the flood destroyed the earth's peoples, effecting a blank slate of sorts for the re-establishment of human civilization. God effected restoration of the story's imbalance by saving Noah's family and allowing them to resettle the earth, ushering in a new era of relationship with God, which included a new covenant (the rainbow and its promises).

Perhaps no story is more poignant than that of Abraham's sacrifice of Isaac (Gen 22). Abraham and Sarah's family was made complete by the birth of Isaac. They viewed him as the fulfillment of God's promise for the building of Abraham's legacy through a nation. God's instruction to Abraham to offer his beloved son as a sacrifice completely threw their lives out of balance. The loss of balance reached a climax at Mount Moriah, as Isaac was trussed up and placed on the altar, with this father's dagger held aloft, ready to be plunged. At that moment, when the imbalance had been struck most starkly, God intervened and restored the balance through the substitute sacrifice, the ram with its horns caught in the bushes.

For Ruth, we barely see her life in balance. We know that she was married to Mahlon, but apparently he died fairly soon, along with his brother and father. Ruth and Naomi shared a life out of balance as they headed to Naomi's homeland to seek food and a livelihood. The imbalance peaked when the famine hit and they were faced with the prospect of starvation. Restoration occurred when Boaz, the kinsman redeemer who finally claimed Ruth as his wife, intervened, restoring her and Naomi to their rightful place within the extended family and caring for their needs.

For Esther, her queenship was thrown off balance when Haman determined to destroy the Jewish people, due to his grudge with Mordecai. The imbalance reached its climax as the day for the slaughter drew near and Esther invited the king and Haman to a feast, where she confronted Haman for his treachery and interceded on behalf of her people, restoring balance as Haman was hanged and those who would have murdered her people were themselves executed.

Job's balanced life was grand, filled with economic and familial prosperity. The balance enjoyed such a tremendous sense of inertia that Satan himself sought to ruin it. Imbalance occurred when Job's prosperity was destroyed, including his children, his properties, and his animals. The imbalance continued to intensify as Job's friends and even his wife piled onto his miseries, urging him to curse God. Restoration occurred when Job finally understood that God's ways are sovereign, at which point God Himself restored in abundance everything that was lost.

More generally, the descendants of Jacob found succor in Egypt as Joseph cared for them through his divinely appointed role in Pharoah's court. Balance was lost, however, little by little when Joseph was forgotten and the Israelites found themselves enslaved. The conditions of their slavery declined until the people cried out to God. The imbalance finds its climax as Moses pled that the pharaoh let the people go, and found an extension in the forty years of wandering in the desert. Restoration occurred in the triumphal entry into the promised land, as God miraculously established His chosen people in their land.

I feel a bit as though I am providing a new version of Hebrews 11, with the "Hall of Restoration" that stretches throughout the Old Testament. As v. 32 says, "And what more can I say? Time is too short." These stories and many more repeat the Restoration Narrative. In these passages we see restoration through a covenant, a sacrificial offering, a kinsman redeemer, an intercessor, a redeemer / friend, a deliverer, each of whom foreshadows the coming Messiah–Restorer. Having said that, I would not be faithful to my proposal if I did not mention that the Restoration Narrative fills the stories of the New Testament as well: Bartimaeus (Mark 10), the woman at the well (John 4), Ananias and Sapphira (Acts 5), the course of the early church, and even the passion week narratives of Christ's crucifixion and resurrection all follow the same patterns. Balance was lost and restored, typically through God's justice and / or loving-kindness.

The Restoration Narrative as Meta-Narrative

Before I begin to apply the Restoration Narrative to more general stories, I should pause for a moment and recognize that I am proposing what might be termed a meta-narrative or meta-allegory for narrative as a whole. Indeed, I am reading an underlying story or metaphor that cuts broadly across many stories, unifying them and centralizing their symbolic meaning under the auspices of a single Story and the accompanying metaphor of God as Author.

Because I trade in literary theory, I am keenly aware of the current aversion to meta-narratives. Certainly, the Restoration Narrative would be called a meta-narrative by most critics since it outlines an explanatory narrative that drives our worldviews. I recognize that the broader academy's hesitation to accept the notion of a meta-narrative is based somewhat on caution. Scholarship is a very careful activity, and broad, sweeping statements are forbidden because they diminish the size and scope of the world. Terms like "all" and "every" imply a completeness of knowledge that is impossible, given how vast the world of human experience is.

Further, there is a strong, almost romantic impulse toward democratizing points of view, making all scholarly claims equally valid, even when it is rationally inappropriate to do so. Scholarly schools are different opinions, the traditional wisdom holds. There is no priority among the critical schools, at least within a reasonable frame of belief. Despite the relative holders of such beliefs, the Marxist has no priority over the Feminist, over the New Critic, over the New Historicist, over the Bakhtinian, and so forth. Each has a place at the table, and each contributes to the conversation among critics.

In the realm of meta-narrative, a number of influential works, from the influential *The Golden Bough* to Joseph Campbell's popular series on myth and humankind, have sought to identify the themes and threads that underlie our stories.

I am, of course, aware of the criticisms leveled by both poststructuralism and postmodernism. I know of Jean-Francois Lyotard's criticisms of anything that smacks of meta-narrative. These criticisms have their points that are well-taken, but simply saying that something is not true is not the same as something *not* being true. As Alister McGrath once observed, "Reality is what you are faced with when you are wrong."[18] In the real world, Jedi mind tricks (*"there is no master narrative"*) do not work. These critics are saying, "There is no master narrative," but what they really are saying is "What *if* there were none of these things?" It may be a fun game to play, but in the real world of narrative, there is more than meets the eye at every turn. Any purely rationalistic approach to narrative always fails because it always fails to consider the inestimable power of the aesthetic elements. Further, many times purely rationalistic approaches also miss the simple fact of the truth that lies in reality.

Truth claims are difficult in our skeptical age. The mantra of our times "What is truth?" is a sentiment that echoes the question asked of Christ by Pontius Pilate in John 18:38. Christ's answer seems to be "The Truth is looking you straight in the face." Perhaps we have a meta-narrative that confronts us on a daily basis as well.

Out-of-hand dismissals of meta-narrative remind me of C. S. Lewis's recollection of a conversation that he had with J. R. R. Tolkien about the grand themes of world literature.[19] Lewis considered this conversation as the final step on his road to conversion to Christianity. Lewis observed to his friend that there was no way that he could accept the truth claims of the faith regarding things like the resurrection because he viewed them as mythological in the worst sense: false and invented in such a way as to communicate a truth but not *the* truth. He recounted the legends of other cultures that fit, in some way, alongside the claims of Christianity. Believing that he had made a critical point, he waited for Tolkien's response.

Tolkien conceded the point that many myths resonate with that of the essentials of Christianity's claims for Christ, but he asked a follow-up question. What if the other myths foreshadowed Christ's coming, that Christ was the incarnation of all of

---

[18] A. McGrath, "Address to CCCU International Forum," CCCU International Forum, Grapevine, TX, April 1, 2006.

[19] Lewis relates this story in "Myth Became Fact," in *God in the Dock,* ed. W. Hooper (Grand Rapids: Eerdmans, 1970), 66–67.

these myths in the truest sense? What if Christ fulfilled a longing that humans felt cross-culturally precisely because it was a God-designed longing?

The question was transformative, for suddenly Lewis found a new way to look at the world's great stories. Instead of dismissing them as contrived efforts that produced artificial meta-narratives that we subconsciously applied to those stories, he began to view the other stories as glimpses of the truth, a divine meta-narrative rooted in the truth of God's own self-revelation of and through Christ. As Lewis himself stated it, "The heart of Christianity is a myth which is also a fact. . . . By becoming fact it does not cease to be myth: that is the miracle. . . . God is more than a god, not less: Christ is more than Balder [a Norse god who parallels Christ's sacrifice], not less."[20]

Lewis then developed his own belief about general revelation and human narrative, wondering if God could not have operated through those "good dreams: I mean those queer stories scattered all through the heathen religions about a god who dies and comes to life again and, by his death, has somehow given new life to men."[21] Missiological folklorist Don Richardson has outlined precisely this scenario in his fascinating *Eternity in Their Hearts*, which detailed a number of culture's traditions that seem to have predicted the coming of the specific beliefs of Christianity.[22] Some of the parallels were startling to be sure.

Critic Louis Markos, pondering the story of Lewis's change of heart, noted,

> If Christianity is true, then the God who created both us and the universe chose to reveal himself through a sacred story that resembles more the imaginative works of epic poets and tragedians than the rational meditations of philosophers and

---

[20] Lewis, "Myth Became Fact," 66–67.

[21] C. S. Lewis, *Mere Christianity* (New York: Macmillan, 1952), 39.

[22] D. Richardson, *Eternity in Their Hearts: Startling Evidence of Belief in the One True God in Hundreds of Cultures throughout the World* (Ventura, CA: Regal, 2006).

theologians. . . . [T]he gospel story spreads its
light both forward and backward to uplift and en-
noble all stories that speak of sacrifice and reconciliation, of messianic promise and eschatological
hope. It was through the Psalms and the Prophets, which were written in poetry, as well as the
"epic" tales of the Old Testament—Abraham's
long, circuitous journey, Joseph and his brothers,
the Passover and Exodus—that Yahweh prepared
the hearts and minds of his people for the incarnation of the Christ. Is it so unbelievable that he
should have used the greatest poets, storytellers
and 'prophets' of antiquity to prepare the hearts
of the pagans?[23]

I would add that these elements that reflect the specific nature of
God, His loving-kindness, His justice, and His glory, may be found
through the application of the lens of the Restoration Narrative in
places far flung. Much of the human narrative tradition reflects the
basics of the gospel: creation, fall, and redemption, as reflected in
the more general balance, imbalance, and restoration.

---

[23] L. Markos, *From Achilles to Christ: Why Christians Should Read the Pagan
Classics* (Downers Grove: IVP Academic, 2007), 249.

5

The Restoration Narrative in Literary Narrative

He restoreth my soul.
                    —Psalm 23:3, KJV

He thown [sic] everything off
balance. If He did what He said,
then it's nothing for you to do
but thow [sic] away everything and
follow Him, and if He didn't, then
it's nothing for you to do but
enjoy the few minutes you got left
the best way you can—by killing
somebody or burning down his house
or doing some other meanness to
him. No pleasure but meanness.

        —Flannery O'Connor, "A Good Man
            Is Hard to Find" (1953)

My father pastored a small Baptist mission church when I was growing up, and we lived at the parsonage, an old farmhouse on several acres of grape vineyards that backed into several hundred acres of farmland and creeks. Our next-door neighbor raised bison and had a small country store. Each afternoon after school I hit the property for a new day of adventures. Saturdays, in particular, included exploring and playing in the nooks and hollows of the seemingly endless landscape. To the west, we could see the lake; on clear days, we could see the freighters making their way to cities like Cleveland and Buffalo. To the east, we could see the hill slopes, which were gorgeous in the winter snow.

The elementary school in town was wonderful, and I adored it. I had many friends and participated in the fine arts programs that were scattered throughout the day. On Fridays, the cafeteria prepared pizzas for lunch; I remember my buddies counting the slices of pepperoni on our small pizzas, competing to see who had the most. Recess was always vigorous. Our teachers were beautiful, or at least were funny, and we had lots of birthday parties at friends' houses. I could write on. When I think back on my childhood, I have almost exclusively fond memories. I remember walking with confidence wherever I went. I was happy almost all the time. In many ways, if I could choose a childhood setting for my own children, it would be just that kind of place.

My childhood was not perfect, of course. I received my share of discipline, I had the usual conflicts at school, and because Dad was a missions pastor, we had nary a penny to spare. When I think back on it, however, it was unlike any other time in my life. My mind turns back to those days with great frequency, especially when I am overwhelmed with work or difficulties. I find a sense of peace in those thoughts.

Old School literary critics would probably call it a time of innocence. I was a child, of course. My memories are tinged with a misty glow that has all but eliminated the darkest of spaces. I was brave. I was creative. I was loved.

The beginning of my life was a lot like the beginning of many stories. There is an excitement, an energy that drives the opening. In some cases, a hopefulness imbues the opening lines. For audiences, personal experience has already taught that such moments will not last. When we read personal narratives like the one I outlined for myself, we always look ahead to the "but" that inevitably comes. "We once were happy, but something happened." This bittersweet understanding of the past creates a sense of empathy through the totality of the human experience. We all know that peace and quiet cannot be sustained in this world. As William Butler Yeats once observed (and Chinua Achebe extended in novel form), "Things fall apart; the center cannot hold."[1] Before the knot can fall apart, however, it must be tied in a state of time that predates the loss of balance.

Paradise: A Time of Balance

One of my favorite stories from world literature is that of *The Rāmāyana*, an epic tale from India that is perhaps the most widely repeated narrative in that culture. Produced in about the fourth century BC by a poet named Vālmīki, *The Rāmāyana* tells the story of Rāma, a prince, who is really an incarnation of Vishnu (one of the chief Hindu gods), who had determined that he needed to provide for humankind a portrait of how to live in the face of suffering. In the story, suffering by an individual can be a part of that person's ultimate redemption from the curse of reincarnation, moving the soul toward transcendence. The tale is epic in scope, and few if any stories in Asia have so persistently influenced culture.

The story's opening outlines the miraculous birth of Rāma and his brothers. Their father, King Dásaratha, rose to prominence, even as his sons grew in strength and reputation. Another king, Janaka, was blessed by the arrival of a beautiful daughter, Sītā, (also through miraculous circumstances), who would one day become Rāma's wife when Rāma won a contest requiring suitors

---

[1] W. B. Yeats, line 3 of "The Second Coming," in *The Norton Anthology of English Literature: The Major Authors,* 6th ed., ed. M. H. Abrams (New York: W. W. Norton, 1996), 2280.

to string a heavy archery bow. Rāma's reputation increased significantly, and his father determined that he would retire from the kingship, allowing Rāma to replace him.

The coronation scene vividly depicts a time of optimism and hope. The people are ecstatic about the impending rise of their beloved prince:

> Women standing at the windows of their houses
> and richly adorned to express their joy, show-
> ered flowers on Rāma. They praised Kausalyā,
> the mother of Rāma; they praised Sītā, Rāma's
> consort. . . . The people rejoiced as if they them-
> selves were being installed on the throne. They
> said to one another: "Rāma's coronation is truly a
> blessing to all the people. While he rules, and he
> will rule for a long time, no one will even have an
> unpleasant experience, or ever suffer."[2]

Rama's impending coronation had united the entire city in an optimistic communion.

At this point, *The Rāmāyana* embodies the overlap between beginning, rising action, and innocence. The beginning of Rāma's initial era of prosperity and young adulthood is at full tide; it has reached the peak of the balance that would define latter longings. The sense of optimism that permeates the early portions of *The Rāmāyana* establishes a benchmark, a time of idyllic memories that will now set the standard for the future. As the story soon hurtles into absolute chaos, there is an implicit longing for that era to be restored.

In that moment, however fleeting, a peace flows throughout the city's residents. Even in Rāma's own apartment, where Sītā awaits his return, there is a hopefulness and optimism that freezes time and establishes a benchmark for joy. More than at any other time, the balance of their way of life is deeply and firmly estab-

---

[2] Swami Venkatesananda, trans., *The Rāmāyana of Vālmīki*, in *Norton Anthology of World Literature*, volume A: *Beginnings to A.D. 100,* 2nd ed., ed. J. W. Clinton (New York: W. W. Norton, 2002), 896.

lished. For the rest of their lives, they would remember that day's festivities and carry that snapshot in their minds until such a time as that peace was restored.

The poignant narration drips with irony, as the audience learns quickly that the balance is about to be upset, with an ensuing chaos hurtling toward the characters. The audience experiences a strong sense of dramatic irony as Rāma makes his way toward the palace for the ceremony, because we know that Kaikeyi has pled her suit for favors from Dasaratha, which includes the forced exile of Rāma into the forest and the establishment of Kaikeyi's own son, Bharata, in the kingly role. Rāma's rise to power and fame are about to be interrupted. As an audience, we know this instinctively, for we know that balance is delicate and cannot last forever. Every step Rāma takes toward the palace complex leads toward the utter loss of innocence. Likewise, every step carries the audience toward the realization that life in this world is more times than not beyond our control. Sometimes conflicts arise from human sins (such as those of Kaikeyi), and sometimes they are thrust on us for reasons beyond our control (such as in the case of Rāma). In all cases, though, the loss of balance creates a more wistful time in our minds.

Not all narratives share such a pristine balance at the beginning. Franz Kafka's *Metamorphosis*, for example, starts off in a dark and depressing world, but quickly matters grow worse as even the dark balance of Gregor Samsa's world is thrown off when he is transformed into a gigantic beetle. In *Oedipus Rex*, the story begins in the middle of a plague, in the midst of the lost balance, but one has to peer fairly far into the past to see when balance was last effected (to some extent in the overthrow of the Sphinx by Oedipus, but more solidly in the time before Oedipus's birth, when Jocasta and Laertes reigned in blissful ignorance of the future). Similarly, in dystopian narratives, like George Orwell's *1984* or Aldous Huxley's *Brave New World* , the time of balance is dimly remembered in the chaos of the story's present times; the very notion of dystopia conveys the idea that something is deeply out of sorts and must be overthrown.

All of us want to experience a moment of balance and stability. Such a moment provides us with halcyon memories that can sustain us during the darkest of our days. It gives us a goal toward which we can strive. When everything around us falls apart, we grow homesick for the peace and order that we once knew. Or that, in the least, we believe can exist. This longing for order was the mission of Mayor Guiliani in the aftermath of the September 11, 2001, attacks on the World Trade Centers; he sought to provide a glimmer of hope that things could be restored to some sort of peace, regardless of how chaotic the moment might be. The epic tradition includes this moment as a part of its basic characteristics: the epic past that is better and somehow better than the present age. Ovid's *Metamorphoses* describes this as the Golden Age, when the world was closer to perfection.

Experience, though, has taught each of us that golden ages cannot last. Eden is not our current setting, even as we long for some sort of return to it as our homeland. Paradise cannot be perpetual; this is not the lot of human existence. Instead, we live in a world of disorder, where reality is the enemy of any kind of lasting peace. Paradise, as John Milton phrased it, has been lost.

Paradise Lost: A Time of Imbalance

The summer after my fifth grade year, I overheard my mother talking on the phone in our living room. The phrase "what are the schools like in the area?" caught my ears so that I began to eavesdrop. She reeled off a series of questions that made it clear even to my ten-year-old mind that she was talking about our family's relocation.

As I said, I loved my youngest years. I was a very happy child. That summer, however, right after Little League season was over, we loaded up a moving truck and headed to Virginia. I was horrified by the move. In some ways, I felt betrayed, and I suppose that I spent the next few years being angry at the world for being plucked away from the woods, my classmates, and even my Little League team. While the folks in Virginia went out of their ways to be nice, and the city's many historical sites intrigued me, I hated living in a suburban neighborhood where I felt boxed in. I did not like the school music program (I had been very active prior to that time). I really did not like my schools at all. I felt, in many ways, as though the proverbial rug had been yanked right out from under me. Everything felt out of balance, as though the idyllic days of my childhood had been lost.

In hindsight, I was being petulant and pouty, but in my mind, that move threw me off kilter. I felt as though my life would never be the same. I still remember one of my last baseball games in New York: the air was sweet, the sun was warm (but not hot), and I had a couple of solid hits and pitched a few good innings. My memory has cemented that evening's game firmly in my memory, and it became a happy place to visit in my imagination when later times were not so great.

Aristotle saw the climax of *Oedipus Rex* as one of the great moments of narrative. Written by Sophocles (c. 496–406 BC) in about 423 BC as a part of a trilogy, *Oedipus Rex* is the golden standard of tragedy. The play begins *in medias res*, as a plague has overtaken the city of Thebes. The people approached their leader, Oedipus, who served as one of three rulers (alongside his wife Jocasta and her brother Creon), hoping that he would be able to save them from the disaster. Immediately, they reminded him that he had once brought order to their city. Oedipus had rescued them from a beast, the sphinx, who had attacked their city, by solving the riddle offered by the beast. At the same time, their previous ruler, Laertes, had been murdered, and when Oedipus displayed his skills with the sphinx, they had offered him the marital hand of Laertes' widow, Jocasta, as a reward. This brief time had brought an era of relative peace, one that at least mimicked the previous time of prosperity under Laertes' previous leadership. That balance had been lost, however, as the plague had grown.

Desperate to solve the situation, Oedipus sent a messenger to the Delphic Oracles, hoping to find the cure for the bleak situation. The word came back that Thebes had given sanctuary to a murderer. Oedipus declared that he would seek out the man and exile him. The story spirals out of Oedipus' control at this point, with each scene revealing more of the horrid truth: Oedipus himself is the murderer, for he is the man who had murdered Laertes. Even worse, he is the child of Laertes and Jocasta; as an infant, he had been cast out into the wilderness because his parents had received a prophecy that their son would murder his father and marry his mother. In an effort to bypass this prophecy, his parents had sought to kill him, only to be thwarted by the kindhearted servant to whom they had given the child.

The original audience already knew the tale. It was very popular in its day, but Sophocles masterfully unfolded the revelation to the characters themselves. One by one, the characters realize the gravity of Oedipus' deed, until even Jocasta runs from the room into her chamber, where she then commits suicide. Sophocles specifically addresses the lost balance of Oedipus' fall; as the ruler teeters on the edge of his ruin, an ironic position given the hobbled nature of his ability to stand upright due to his long-injured feet, his brother-in-law Creon declares, "You've lost your sense of balance" (line 616). The reality of his guilt then confronts Oedipus with the crimes of both patricide and incest. The scene is pitiable when he goes into Jocasta's chamber and scratches out his own eyes before returning to the stage with bloody cheeks.

Since the beginning of the play, when Oedipus boasts, "You pray to the gods? Let me grant your prayers,"[3] the audience has the sensation of falling down an elevator shaft, dropping quickly and uncontrollably until the bottom is reached, halting just prior to what would be a shattering impact, only to feel jolted and unnerved by the experience. At this moment, Oedipus embodies the overlapping of middle, climax, and experience. The middle portion of the narrative has reached its fulfillment. The emotional investment of the audience can no longer bear further revelations. The chaos has peaked so that we are left weeping for the man who had shared the hubris of his parents, believing that he could outsmart the plans for his life that had been described by the gods. His arrogance placed him in a position where he could finally learn from his experiences and realize his proper place in a chaotic universe.

---

[3] *Oedipus the King,* line 245.

At this moment, the audience longs for a restoration of peace, an inbursting of justice. When Oedipus' daughter, Antigone, joins him, prepared to help lead him into his period of exile, we feel an odd sort of optimism that somehow even Oedipus, in spite of his own sins, will endure and somehow live out his days in a kind of weakened peace. More importantly, his realization confronts the audience with a realization of their own: humans must submit themselves to the will of the gods through humility.

The climax's peak, the moment when the protagonist's experiences have reached their maximum point, might be called the "epiphany." Originally a religious term, twentieth-century writers such as James Joyce used the term to describe the moment when the character meets the truth. In Joyce's short story "Araby," for example, the main character realizes the vanity of his puerile fantasies about his friend's older sister, whose beauty has enraptured him, and leaves the bazaar shattered by the reality that life is empty and meaningless, without transcendence or hope.[4] The epiphany, however, was a new term, not a new experience. In *The Gilgamesh Epic*, the protagonist had his epiphany when his best friend Enkidu died a lingering death. Gilgamesh refused to leave the corpse until it began to be maggot-ridden, at which time his servants dragged him away. In that moment, he realized for the first time in his life that he was not immortal. In spite of his semi-divine nature, he would die as well. That moment threw his life completely out of balance and set him off on a quest to seek eternal life.

To some extent, the depth (or height) of the climax of experience is relative to the intensity of the peace from the time of balance. When I think on my dissatisfaction with my post-move life, I can remember wishing ironically that my childhood had not been so peaceful, for if it had not have been, perhaps the frustrations I had over school and our suburban lifestyle might have been more tolerable. If ignorance were bliss, I thought, then perhaps I would have been more blissful if I had not have had such positive experiences in my younger days. In the same way, classical tragedies

---

[4] J. Joyce, "Araby," in *The Heath Introduction to Literature,* 6th ed., ed. A. S. Landry (Lexington, MA: Heath, 1988), 300–306.

strike us as more moving when we see a great person fall. More recent narratives focus on the grief we feel when we see the imbalance that comes to the life of someone who is more like us, creating in us a sense of "but for the grace of God, there go I" as the saying goes. In all cases, the chaos of imbalance, the sting of experience, the horror of the epiphany's realization resonate with each of us, for all of our lives are precarious at best.

As stories depict their imbalance, the audience finds itself longing for resolution. Our interest is piqued in how the outcome will arise. We crave something to come out of the conflict. In the best examples of narrative, our own anxieties over the ending come to the surface, quickening our pulse and riveting our attention. We cannot imagine how unsatisfying the story would be without a final resolution.

Most of us have experienced this feeling: when we watch a television show and realize that there is no way that the story can be resolved in the time left, we know that a "to be continued" notice is about to occur. I can remember watching such a show in the television lounge of my college dorm, and people yelling at the screen when those words appeared. Likewise, authors know how to manipulate this desire. Perhaps the most famous example is in Miguel Cervantes' *Don Quixote*, when the narrator built up a battle scene between the title character and a "choleric Biscayan."[5] As the two men hurtle toward each other, swords drawn and ready for blood, the narrator bursts in and declares that he does not know the end of the story: the rest of the original source of the tale had been lost. For pages, then, the narrator describes his own frustration with this lack of an ending, and how he stumbled onto a new manuscript, in Arabic of all things, that picked up the story once again. Now, after an extended interruption, the story could move from its climax into a state of resolution. The suspended imbalance was released and directed once again toward restoration.

---

[5] M. Cervantes, *Don Quixote*, in *The Norton Anthology of World Literature*, vol. C: *1500 to 1650,* 2nd ed., trans. S. Putnam (New York: W. W. Norton, 2002), 2700.

Paradise Regained:
A Time of Restoration

I suppose that most Christians have points in their lives when God has caught their attention and convicted them of their egocentrism. This is not a conversion experience but rather a quickening of spirit, an increased sense of God's righteousness. The turning point in my own pilgrimage to find restoration came in an odd way. My sense of angst came and went, but I had grown dissatisfied with the instability of my emotions. One day I went to see the film adaptation of Somerset Maugham's novel *The Razor's Edge*. I watched the movie's careful depiction of the importance of making peace with our lot in life and was startled by the sense of peace that the main character, Larry Darrell, developed. While the Maugham story exalted Eastern philosophy's emphasis on inner peace, I found myself deeply convicted that the peace of Christ was not residing in my heart in the way that it should. I found both comfort and conviction in the words of 2 Tim 2:22: "Flee from youthful passions, and pursue righteousness, faith, love, and peace, along with those who call on the Lord from a pure heart." Repenting of my attitude, I cried out for God to restore to me the joy of my salvation and to bring balance back to my heart. I understood afresh the words of David in Ps 51:12: "Restore the joy of Your salvation to me, and give me a willing spirit."

The deep longing produced by imbalance expresses itself in a variety of ways. The quest for resolution, for satisfaction, is powerful and in some ways overwhelming. Some narratives propose that the answer may be a kind of resignation about the place of humankind in the chaotic world (embracing the imbalance). Others propose solutions that are rooted in materialism (wealth, sensuality, etc.). The establishment of a lasting legacy may suffice in some viewpoints, and a release from the human realm through the assumption of divinity is a further option in still other narratives. Each of these, of course, satisfies only partially.

The oldest extant epic poem is *The Epic of Gilgamesh*, telling about the legendary king of Uruk who ruled circa 2700 BC. The earliest complete copy of the poem dates to circa 600 BC.

This masterpiece of the Sumerian and Akkadian cultures provides a glimpse into the cultural background of some of the earliest Old Testament passages.

Gilgamesh had been born as a god-king: he was two-thirds divine and one-third mortal. He was handsome, strong, and intelligent, the embodiment of the abstract ideal of human kingship. He also, however, possessed a prodigious ego that caused him to terrorize the people in his kingdom.

A goddess tried to correct this arrogance by creating Enkidu, who was part animal and part human. Enkidu was Gilgamesh's foil, a challenger who cannot be overcome by his strength. Quickly, the two bonded and set out on a series of adventures. Gilgamesh, however, insulted the goddess Ishtar, who determined to punish him. A series of further adventures led to the death of Enkidu, which devastated Gilgamesh. Death reminded the protagonist of his own mortality (the death song he sings for his lost friend is almost humorously self-centered), so he determined to travel to the land of Utnapishtim the Faraway, who had survived the global flood and had been assigned immortality by the gods. While imbalance came to the kingdom when Gilgamesh assumed the throne, imbalance came to Gilgamesh personally when his mortality dissolved his sense of superiority.

The hero's horror at discovering his mortality created in him a longing for the one thing he did not possess: complete immortality. As he traveled to seek this prize, several characters confronted him with the same message: "When the gods created man they allotted to him death, but life they retained in their own keeping. As for you, Gilgamesh, fill your belly with good things; day and night, night and day, dance and be merry, feast and rejoice. Let your clothes be fresh, bathe yourself in water, cherish the little child that holds your hand, and make your wife happy in your embrace; for this too is the lot of man."[6]

---

[6] *The Epic of Gilgamesh*, in *The Norton Anthology of World Literature*, vol. A: *Beginnings to A.D. 100,* 2nd ed., trans. N. K. Sandars (New York: W. W. Norton, 2002), 32–33.

After failing a final test involving a serpent and a lotus blossom, Gilgamesh realized that he was impotent to change his fate. He resolved to live out his life in humility. His resignation to his fate restored balance to his own life; his determination to rule humbly restored balance to the kingdom as a whole.

To some extent, this ending is satisfying, in that it restores justice to the kingdom. No longer do the people suffer at the hands of Gilgamesh. In the long term, however, the ending is a frustrating reminder of just how temporary all resolutions are. Gilgamesh may have learned his lesson, but experience tells us that other rulers will rule autocratically in the future, repeating the sins of the former ruler. Even worse, Gilgamesh dies, just as will everyone in the audience. The story's depictions of the afterlife are not very attractive, in fact, and serve as a kind of warning that this world is the one where life occurs; once life ends, nothing can bypass the effects of death, including the decay of the body. Nothing can be permanent.

Especially impermanent and dissatisfying are the solutions offered by the materialists. Fitzgerald's *The Great Gatsby* portrays the vanity of material solutions in a potent way. This pursuit of romantic redemption is what drove the main character: Jimmy Gatz reconstructed himself as Jay Gatsby, building an immense fortune and covertly pursuing his lost love, Daisy Buchanan. As Gatsby finally presented himself to Daisy, he tried to overwhelm her with his immense wealth by giving her a tour of his immense mansion. In his bedroom, he showed her a cabinet that contained an incredible collection of hand-tailored shirts in unimaginable colors. Together they began to fling the shirts around the room, until Daisy broke down crying, stating that she had never seen such a beautiful sight. At that moment, Gatsby believed that his love had now been requited and his pursuit made complete. This false sense of restoration, however, does not last, as the story spirals into chaos, ending in the accidental death of Myrtle Wilson and Gatsby's murder at the hands of Myrtle's husband, George. Despite his great wealth, Gatsby's life ended violently, and the other characters were confronted with the emptiness of life's pursuits, whether of pleasure or prosperity.

In Shakespeare's poetry, a shadow narrative can be constructed in some of his sonnets. These brief poems tap into a number of traditions about the building of legacies through art. One of the most famous of all Latin sayings was *ars longa, tempus breve*, which is to say, more or less, "art lasts, though time (life) is short." Art, then, is a way to generate immortality of a kind, through the creation of a legacy. Sonnet 18 celebrates the power of the poet to grant eternal life to his beloved: "But thy eternal summer shall not fade . . . / So long as men can breathe or eyes can see, / So long lives this and this gives life to thee" (lines 9, 13–14).[7] A similar sentiment is shared in John Keats' "Ode on a Grecian Urn": "When old age shall this generation waste, / Thou shalt remain, in midst of other woe / Than ours, a friend to man" (lines 46–48).[8] While these poems are not long narratives, they communicate the desire of the author to produce something that will transcend this world: art that lasts.

Even this solution is unsatisfying, however, because the balance that is restored due to the threat of death is not one that the author can enjoy: it gives hope during the writer's life, but it cannot stave off death itself. The only hope for defeating death is through the process of apotheosis.

The pinnacle of the secular impulse toward restoration is probably that of *apotheosis*, the translation of a protagonist into divine status. Apotheosis has been present in many cultures and, in fact, shows up in American folk mythology in the fresco painted inside the dome of the U. S. Capital Building in Washington, DC, which depicts a symbolic apotheosis of George Washington. The most famous apotheosis is probably that of Julius Caesar, which is found in *The Aeneid* and in Ovid's *Metamorphoses*. A prophecy declares that a descendant of Aeneas will one day be translated into a shooting star.

---

[7] W. Shakespeare, "Sonnet 18," in *The Riverside Shakespeare* (Dallas: Houghton Mifflin, 1974), 1752.

[8] J. Keats, "Ode on a Grecian Urn," in *The Norton Anthology of English Literature: The Major Authors,* ed. M. H. Abrams (New York: W. W. Norton, 1996), 1793–95.

This longing for a permanent restoration, to be a new creation that transcends the rest of translation, reflects the temporality from which most restoration suffers. We long not only for the restoration of balance, but for the loss of balance that repeats itself endlessly in this world, to be disrupted permanently. We know that peace will end and that prosperity will be short-lived in this world, so we long for our own translation into the world of eternity, not as gods but rather as saints in heaven: "Listen! I am telling you a mystery: We will not all fall asleep, but we will all be changed, in a moment, in the blink of an eye, at the last trumpet. For the trumpet will sound, and the dead will be raised incorruptible, and we will be changed. For this corruptible must be clothed with incorruptibility, and this mortal must be clothed with immortality" (1 Cor 15:51–53).

In this way, Christ is reconciling all things to Himself (Col 1:20) in eternity, restoring balance to the universe that was lost in Eden and effected at Calvary. This balance is the rest, the peace, and the merciful justice for which we long in so many of our stories. Christ's reconciliation of all things provides not only history with a teleological direction; it creates a spiritual teleology as well: our spirits crave the restoration of a relationship with God. Augustine noted in the *Confessions*: "For Thou hast made us for Thyself and our hearts are restless til they rest in Thee."[9] With Blaise Pascal famously extending this idea as well, both men describe the internal, deep craving that each person feels concerning a sense of completion. Even in pagan ideas about the soul, such as the Platonic notion of the soul's different parts, there is a deep search for something that completes or enhances one's eternal essence. Narrative imbalance confronts us with the imbalance of our own souls. Intuitively, we know that something is awry. We long to have our imbalance restored to a position of balance, and in our spirits, we sense that nothing that is a part of this world can truly satisfy. For those who embrace the completion offered through Christ, the restoration is effected wholly. For those who reject the possibility

---

[9] Augustine, *Confessions,* trans. F. J. Sheed (Lanham MD: Sheed and Ward, 1944), 1.

of such a restoration, there is an endless angst that drives their spirits even through their rejection. This is, I believe, part of what stands behind the post-Enlightenment rejection of the final stage of the Restoration Narrative; if the metaphysical does not exist, then restoration is not possible. Obsession, then, results from the maintenance of the imbalance, a sort of reveling that mimics the words of Christopher Marlowe's Mephistophilis, when asked why he tries to steal others' souls: *"Solamen miseris socios habuisse doloris"* ("Misery loves company").[10] Recent drama, in particular, has a tendency to avoid resolution. "Life has no easy resolutions" is the rally cry of these writers. While that may be true, the fact that there are no easy resolutions reflects the incredible desire for satisfaction that we all feel; there is no amelioration of the desire through the simple avoidance of its satisfaction.

Audiences feel restless as the narrative drives inexorably toward its climax; this restlessness echoes the very restlessness of the soul itself. For Christians, this restlessness resonates deeply with the basic sensibilities of the faith itself. Because we are fallen, we have become incomplete apart from God. Augustine crystallized that sense of imperfection in his own writings, declaring it out of his own restlessness in the midst of wandering. God not only completes our loneliness but the default, broken state of our souls.

Narrative and General Revelation

As I discussed previously, three elements seem to provide the foundation for general revelation's depiction of God: His creative agency, His loving-kindness, and His justice.

His creative agency seems to be understood best in terms of how little control we have over the world and even our lives. Sometimes the world is chaotic because it just *is* chaotic, and sometimes it is chaotic because of our own actions. Most of us can empathize with Paul's lament that he cannot control even himself; he is not making a claim that he is exempt from moral culpability for his actions, but rather admitting that he is a selfish, broken creature.

---

[10] C. Marlowe, *Doctor Faustus* (New York: Signet, 2001), 2.1.43.

His loving-kindness is expressed in the constant human desire to find love, to love and be loved. The heart is restless; it contains a God-shaped void. It longs deeply for restored relationship.

His justice is expressed in our desire for right and wrong to be upheld. Even as we empathize with Oedipus because each of us has tried to pursue our own wishes over and against those of the divine, we celebrate that a man who has committed both patricide and incest has been brought to justice.

Each of us senses that something has been lost and that we need something that will restore that to us. If, as modern thinking tells us, there is no restoration possible, then we are left with only Epicurean delights, Stoic resignation, or Absurdist suicidal tendencies. Perhaps no more poignant depiction of this can be found than that of Flannery O'Connor in "A Good Man Is Hard to Find."[11] An escaped serial killer, The Misfit, holds a family hostage, finally murdering each of them in turn. Panic-stricken, the grandmother cries out to Jesus for protection. The Misfit thinks she is cursing, however, and joins her in complaining about Jesus:

> Jesus thown (sic) everything off balance. It was the same case with Him as with me except He hadn't committed any crime and they could prove I had committed one because they had the papers on me. . . . Jesus was the only One that ever raised the dead, . . . and He shouldn't have done it. He thown everything off balance. If He did what He said, then it's nothing for you to do but thow [sic] away everything and follow Him, and if He didn't, then it's nothing for you to do but enjoy the few minutes you got left the best way you can—by killing somebody or burning down his house or doing some other meanness to him. No pleasure but meanness.[12]

---

[11] F. O'Connor, "A Good Man Is Hard to Find," in *The Heath Introduction to Literature,* 6th ed., ed. A. S. Landry (Lexington, MA: Heath, 1988), 397–410.
[12] O'Connor, "A Good Man," 408–9.

This is the avoidance of restoration distilled into one universal character, reacting to the so-called "Trilemma Dilemma" as articulated by C. S. Lewis: Christ was a liar, a lunatic, or lord. The first two mean that there is no hope in this world and that Christianity is fraudulent. The latter means that we must submit to His Lordship. Like most persons, The Misfit refuses to "thow [sic] away everything and follow Him," so he resorts to a twisted Epicureanism that finds pleasure in sadism. He knows, however, that he is damned for his refusal and determines to share his misery with others. Avoidance of restoration intensifies the imbalance that characters and real persons feel. Much of the misery and brokenness in the world results from the avoidance of the ultimate restoration offered by Christ, for such a restoration has ramifications: Christ is revealed as Truth personified. And His Story, then, is true.

I know a man who resisted this restoration for much of his young life. In his literature classes at a large state university, "Bill" enjoyed studying medieval and Renaissance poetry.[13] He was a self-confessed atheist who thought that Christianity was just one more of the world's mythologies, with no grounding in truth. In fact, he believed that religious belief was a sign of either mental weakness or instability.

As his professors made their way through the various poems, Bill found himself becoming curious about the sense of justice that he started noticing in the stories. Despite his lack of trust in religion, he still had a highly developed sense of right and wrong. He believed that each person determines what is right or wrong for himself and that the best of persons try to do what is right as much of the time as is possible.

As he read the great narratives, he told me that he was shocked at how much murder, lust, and destruction could be found in history, and so little justice or even good. Something caused him to begin to reflect on this in his own personal life. He suddenly began to feel that his own moral compass was out of balance. Like the

---

[13] This is one story of many I have heard about persons who have found faith during their experience with literature. In this case, I knew the man personally, and he told me the details himself. I have tried to be faithful to what he told me.

characters in the stories that he had read, he saw himself as terribly flawed. This moved him deeply.

He told me later that he knew in his heart that it was wrong to lie and to be jealous. He had tried to be a moral rationalist, believing rather stoically that his good works could outweigh his misdeeds and create for himself a legacy of kindness and good reputation. In the end, though, as he meditated on just how hard this was, he realized that he failed more than he succeeded in keeping his own moral code. What is more, when he read about persons like Mother Teresa or the saints of medieval history, he was struck by just how sacrificial their lives had been in terms of service to humanity.

The biggest blow, however, came from reading Milton's *Paradise Lost*.[14] When he read about how The Son (Jesus) interceded on behalf of Adam and Eve (Book X), preparing to take on Himself the punishment for the sins that humankind had committed, Bill was awestruck by such a view that someone else might shoulder the burdens of other persons' moral failings. He knew, he said, for the first time in his life that Christianity had a different view of life and morality than did the other worldviews he had studied.

As Bill began talking about this with some of his friends who were Christians, he decided to embrace the truth of the Christian vision of the world. He gave up trying to do it all by himself and began to follow Christ. Soon he was deeply involved in the life of a local faith community. The start of his conversion process, however, was in a nonchurch setting. The start of his understanding was through the reflections of special revelation and even the Incarnation that were found in narrative poetry. His new life in Christ began through his readings of old stories.

---

[14] J. Milton, *Paradise Lost,* in *The Complete Poetry of John Milton,* ed. J. T. Shawcross (New York: Anchor, 1973), 249–518.

6

How Then Shall
We Deal with
Narrative?

For God was pleased [to have] all
His fullness dwell in Him, and
through Him to reconcile everything
to Himself by making peace through
the blood of His cross—whether
things on earth or things in heaven.
                    —Colossians 1:19-20

I n the post-September 11th travel world, heading to the airport to catch a flight is no longer a last-minute activity. I live about two hours from the airport where I usually depart, and I always allow at least an extra hour of travel time in case of traffic. I add another hour and a half for the possible line at check in and for Homeland Security, and, of course, a generous cushion of time for the walk down to the gate. This means that most of the time I have at least two hours of sitting in the terminal, which aggravates me to no end. I have my ticket, my luggage is in the system, and I am ready to go, but the departure time has not yet arrived. More times than not, I sit in the terminal thinking, "I'm so tired of waiting!" I become patient, however, when I remember that even though the precautions are aggravating in the moment, they are worthwhile in the long run.

Much of our lives is spent waiting: in line, at stoplights, for phone calls, for good or bad news. Patience is not a strong suit for most persons. We want resolution *now*; we want everything *right this moment.* Poet John Milton was no exception to this. In his famous Sonnet 19, he noted that he was weary of being blind, for he longed to feel useful and to fulfill what he viewed as his divine calling: writing. In a pique, he voiced his frustrations, only to be confronted by Patience personified, who chided his impatience, reminding him, "They also serve who only stand and wait" (line 14).[1] My late pastor Frank Pollard once observed that being a Christian servant is a lot like being a restaurant waiter: most of our lives are spent preparing for just a few moments actually spent serving face-to-face.

The challenge, then, is to figure out what to do with our lives while we await the coming of Christ. The question is, "How shall we live in the meantime?" Francis Schaeffer asked, "How Should We Then Live?"[2] Charles Colson and Nancy Pearcey asked, "How

---

[1] J. Milton, "Sonnet 19," in *The Complete Poetry of John Milton,* rev. ed., ed. J. T. Shawcross (New York: Anchor, 1973), 243–44.

[2] F. A. Schaeffer, *How Should We Then Live? The Rise and Decline of Western Thought and Culture*, 50th anniversary edition (Wheaton, IL: Crossway, 2005).

Now Shall We Live?"[3] Each of us must ask such a question: now that we have submitted ourselves to the lordship of Christ, how are we to live in the meantime? While history moves toward its final fulfillment in the Second Coming, life goes on.

The creation–fall–redemption framework that Christian apologists employ is not the end of the quest for understanding the gospel. Our redemption is made complete in Christ, even as it will be made complete on the day of judgment. A fourth stage of the framework helps us to understand how the other three stages find application in our lives: mission. The mission stage, also called "consummation" or "restoration," is rooted in Christ's work of reconciliation in our world. Beyond redemption, which is the renewal of the imbalance that sin effected, there is a reconciliation of all brokenness to Christ and through Christ. As Col 1:19–20 makes clear, He seeks "to reconcile everything to Himself," and not just things in the human realm; Christ reconciles all things, whether "things on earth or things in heaven." In this way, He guides us in the way that we now live, effecting reconciliation as His agents. Now that we have had our balance restored, we are a part of Christ's ministry of restoration for the brokenness of nature, human relationships, and others' relationships with God Himself. As Colson and Pearcey state it, "We are called to bring these principles into every area of life and create a new culture. Equipped with this understanding, . . . Christians can take up spiritual arms in the great cosmic struggle between conflicting worldviews."[4] This is our mission.

Our mission may be understood evangelistically (in our calling to bear witness to the gospel), interpersonally (in our imperatives to effect community), or vocationally (in our leading as to

---

[3] C. Colson and N. Pearcey, *How Now Shall We Live?* (Wheaton: Tyndale House, 1999).

[4] Colson and Pearcey, *How Now Shall We Live?*, 36–37. Andy Crouch, in *Culture Making,* extends this call to action by exhorting Christians to create culture that engages society in vigorous and comely ways: "The risk in thinking 'worldviewishly' is that we will start to think that the best way to change culture is to analyze it. . . . But culture is not changed simply by thinking" (Andy Crouch, *Culture Making: Recovering our Creative Calling* [Downers Grove: IVP, 2008], 64.

how we might live out our faith, either as a means of livelihood or as an avocational pursuit). Our lives are bound by the twofold imperative of the Great Commandment and the Great Commission. As an educator, I cannot help but point out that these two passages are linked by the life of the mind: "Love the Lord your God . . . with all your mind" (Mark 12:30) and "make disciples of all the nations . . . teaching them" (Matt 28:19–20). Our mission is in part an intellectual mission, one in which "though we live in the body, we do not wage war in an unspiritual way, since the weapons of our warfare are not worldly, but are powerful through God for the demolition of strongholds. We demolish arguments and every high-minded thing that is raised up against the knowledge of God, taking every thought captive to obey Christ" (2 Cor 10:3–4). This mission urges us to avoid being "conformed to this age, but [to] be transformed by the renewing of your mind, so that you may discern what is the good, pleasing, and perfect will of God" (Rom 12:2).

All of this means that part of our mission is the application of the mind of Christ (1 Cor 2:16) to human intellectual pursuits. We are agents of reconciliation, even in the realm of the intellect. This is true particularly in the realm of narrative.

In my literature courses, I constantly strive to draw parallel connections between the stories and real life. I know men who have experienced temptations similar to those of Gawain and Aeneas. I have known women who were falsely accused like Sita and Isabella. I have known leaders who acted like Cassius and Iago, even as I have known others who were manipulated like Brutus and Othello. The connections are what keep narratives alive: we can learn from the experiences of the past because they are *human* experiences. Narrative continues to be applicable, just as it is beautiful and influential.

When I stress this applicability, I am emphasizing that narrative should not be relegated to past importance. It does not belong in a box of cultural relics, brought out to be looked over but then stowed away like a prom corsage. It continues to urge us toward lives of reflection and grace.

If we take note of the Restoration Narrative and then declare, "Neat!" but put the concept up on a shelf to be forgotten, then we have sealed narrative in a tomb of irrelevance. The life of faith, however, is one of constant application. Orthodoxy means nothing without orthopraxy; faith without works is, as Jas 2:26 reminds us, dead. Thought without application is a waste of understanding.

For those of us who are passionate about narrative, a final step is necessary. The Restoration Narrative leads to a calling to consider narrative in a way that is redemptive: we are called to read redemptively. What's more, it leads those who produce narrative to do likewise: to write redemptively.

Milton is instructive at this point once again. At the conclusion of his epic *Paradise Lost*, he describes Adam and Eve's expulsion from the garden as both terrifying and optimistic. As they turned to walk away from the only home they had known, they asked the question that each of us must face: "How shall we live in the meantime?" Milton's description of their first steps is poignant and inspiring: "The World was all before them, where to choose / Thir [sic] place of rest, and Providence thir guide: / They hand in hand with wandring steps and slow, / Through *Eden* took thir solitarie way" (lines 646–649).[5]

With the Restoration Narrative as our guide, then, and narrative itself bonding our hands together, let us turn now to explore how the mission of the mind might be applied in ways that are both hopeful and purposeful.

---

[5] J. Milton, *Paradise Lost,* in *The Complete Poetry of John Milton,* ed. J. T. Shawcross (New York: Anchor, 1973), 517.

7

Reading
Redemptively

God gave these four young men
knowledge and understanding in
every kind of literature and
wisdom. . . . In every matter of
wisdom and understanding that the
king consulted them about, he found
them 10 times better than all the
diviner-priests and mediums in his
entire kingdom

—Daniel 1:17,20

———————

"Take it and read! Take
it and read!"

—Augustine (c. AD 398), <u>Confessions</u>

One of my relatives had a terrible first day of kindergarten. She had looked forward to attending school and was nervous, of course, but when she got home, she burst into tears. Her mother asked her what was wrong, and she lamented, "They didn't teach me how to read!"

I think that most parents long to see their children become readers at an early age. Nothing warms my own heart quite so much as hearing my kids beg to have ten more minutes to read before they turn off their lights at bedtime.

Regrettably, though, something tends to happen as children grow into adulthood: they stop reading. Somehow reading has a tendency to become relegated to being a childhood activity, or worse yet, a school activity that should be unburdened from our lives. In 2007, one quarter of U. S. adults reported that they had not read a single book during the year.[1] I suspect that this survey means that at least another quarter of the population probably said they did but lied.

Neil Postman famously claimed that we have decided to entertain ourselves to death. We love stories as a certainty, but we watch narratives now more than we read them. We do enjoy good narratives, however, especially in the blending of narrative and nonfiction, such as in the masterful writings of David McCullough and others.

The aforementioned 2007 survey noted that churchgoers read only half as many books as nonchurchgoers. While American culture in general often reveals a deep crisis of intellect, for Christians in particular, this is a problem. Religious publishing categories have enjoyed success over the past couple of decades, even as the content of much of that publishing is less than challenging and in many cases treats faith in ways that are likewise less than adequate. Most Christians are not readers, and many of those who are readers lack discernment in how they approach narrative.

---

[1] "One in Four Americans Read No Books Last Year," Manchester *Guardian*, August 22, 2007. http://www.guardian.co.uk/books/2007/aug/22/news (accessed May 2, 2009).

The life of the mind is one of the most important tools that Christians have with which to worship and serve God. Christ Himself underscored the role of our intellects when he answered the rich young ruler with a clarion call to a fully integrated life in the Greatest Commandment. Leading a life that is fully dedicated to the glory of God, that is devotional in every aspect, includes the employment of our minds to the exploration of God even through the way that we approach narrative.

In my introductory literature classes, I always give my students a piece of advice on writing successful essays: Do not just identify the facts of the story; explain *why* the facts are so, including how those facts might affect our thinking or our behavior. "Don't just identify; explain why" goes my shorthand rule of thumb.

As I have pondered the effects of the Restoration Narrative, I have been convinced that the question should not simply end there, with the identification of such a principle. Our ability to see the gospel in stories should have ramifications for how we think, how we explore God's revelation of Himself, and how we see the rest of the world. Our mission as thinking Christians who seek to love God with our minds should find expression in the way that we read.

Cultivating a Love for Story

Because my father was a pastor, church activities filled most of his evenings. My parents were dogmatic, however, about having a daily meal together as a family, so we almost always ate breakfast together at our small kitchen table. Usually, we would eat cold cereal or some other relatively quick food, and then we would have our family devotional. We would read a chapter or so from the Bible, review the missionaries' birthdays from a small booklet provided by our denomination, and pray for various things.

The Bible we used was oversized and squarish, with a sort of navy blue cover. I loved flipping the pages to look at the scattered illustrations that made it "child friendly." They were simple line drawings. I remember thinking frequently that there weren't enough of them.

Being Southerners, my family was filled with a love for story. I remember absolutely loving the stories that fill the Bible: the stories about Noah, Abraham, Daniel, and David. Even the gross incident where Jael drives the tent peg through the temple of Sisera (Judges 4) fired my imagination.

When our twins were born, my wife and I received a number of children's books. From a very early time in their lives, we developed a bedtime routine that included reading from these books. A few were just sweet, soothing stories, but our favorites were in the *Read-Aloud Bible Stories* series by Ella K. Lindvall, which include wonderful illustrations by H. Kent Puckett.[2] On most nights, the kids would beg to hear these stories. I personally believe that a part of their current love of story and reading is directly attributable to this bedtime ritual.

At some point we switched to reading from an actual Bible. We got the children their own "big kids'" Bibles to take to church and to read themselves. During our evening prayers, we have tried a variety of readings, from chapters in the Bible to character-building books to a children's catechism. In our household, bedtime always means a time of sharing and a prayer to end the day.

As I visited with a dear friend and his family some time ago, he asked his guests to participate in their family altar when his children's bedtimes came. They employed a children's catechism with their very young children. It was heartwarming to hear their ability to memorize the appropriate responses to the questions, which were either scriptural or patterned on Scripture. I was reminded about how most adults greatly underestimate the memorization skills of children.

When I returned home, I pondered the difference between that family altar and the ones my family had completed when my children were that age. Ours were based on Bible stories; theirs were based on didactic theology. While our devotionals had not included memorization of specific important Scripture passages

---

[2] E. K. Lindvall, *Read-Aloud Bible Stories* (Chicago: Moody, 1988–95). This is a four-volume series.

and theirs had, our experiences did create a strong memory of the various stories that fill the pages of the Old and New Testaments.

The more I reflect on how we teach the Bible and theology, the more I think that adults, especially theologically inclined adults, tend to err on the side of teaching theology as a narrowly confined set of verses and facts. The reverse is true, that many adults, especially narratively inclined adults, tend to err on the side of teaching the stories without making application of their deeper meanings.

I have noticed over the years that many pastors are guilty of doing the same things. Many are fabulous storytellers who can make the Bible's narratives come to life, but in the end, there is an overly simplified meaning that is detached from the overarching theological themes of the Word. Others stew the life out of the text, performing the almost miraculous feat of turning God's Word into a boring string of clauses. Both extremes miss the goal of communicating the Scriptures through means of application, which connects the Word with people's lives.

Surely there is a balance to be struck between the Bible's narratives and its more stripped-down theologically driven verses.[3] When we emphasize story to the exclusion of theology, we end up with mushy beliefs that tend to be driven by our own ideas rather than a coherent understanding of Scripture. Novelist William Faulkner once observed that his love for the Bible was planted at the breakfast table, when his grandfather required everyone to quote a verse before eating.[4] Faulkner grew to love the Old

---

[3] Even the books of the New Testament that may appear to be the least narrative, the Epistles, are, in fact, the *products* of what might be described as narrative: each was written to meet the specific concerns and needs of a particular church context. Surely, there are stories that stand behind Paul's warnings about having affairs with stepmothers and so forth. I highly recommend R. E. Brown's *The Community of the Beloved Disciple* (New York: Paulist, 1979), which reconstructs the story behind John's epistles. *Community* is not a story *per se*, but it reveals the subtle story that John relates to us. Every portion of the Scriptures is both tied to God's overarching story of grace and redemption and to the specific narrative context of the original audiences.

[4] For a discussion of the biblical influences on Faulkner's fiction, see G. Meeter's "Bible," in *A William Faulkner Encyclopedia,* ed. R. W. Hamblin and C. A. Peek (Santa Barbara, CA: Greenwood, 1999), 40–41.

Testament in particular, eschewing much of the New Testament as not being very interesting. For him, the Bible was a wellspring of stories that had power, even as he never embraced the theological implications of the stories as a whole. Surely, there is an incomplete understanding of biblical narrative present there, but exalting theology over narrative likewise produces a hobbled hermeneutic. As Mark Bertrand has observed, "We should not emphasize story to the exclusion of all else . . . but we must restore it to an equal footing, to rehabilitate it, and to ask why Christians, with so many exalted examples to draw upon, should not once more become the champions of imagination."[5]

For people who call themselves "The People of the Book," most Christians do not read the Bible very much. We talk about it, we sermonize about it, we even read other books about it, but we spend precious little time actually reading it. Worse, we rarely read the Bible's actual stories once we reach adulthood. In fact, professional Christians such as pastors may be the guiltiest about this. Reading secondary texts about the Bible is no substitute for reading the Bible itself. John North once reported that students in his Literature and the Bible class had complained, "Sir, in the Religious Studies program we could only find courses on various views about the Bible; we could find none in which we could read and study the Bible itself."[6] Ministers, in particular, who rediscover the stories of the Bible may find that they help the text come back to life. I am afraid that most of us live similarly, in agreement with the Bible, even as we live at a distance from it. It is on a pedestal, exalted and foundational to what we do, but we do not read it as often as we should or in some of the ways that we should.

J. R. R. Tolkien wrote what is perhaps the most influential essay ever written on the epic poem *Beowulf.* In that essay, he lambasted how the critics of his day had squeezed all of the magic out of the text. He scolded them for being "embarrassed" by its supernatural

---

[5] J. M. Bertrand, *(Re)Thinking Worldview: Learning to Think, Live and Speak in This World* (Wheaton, IL: Crossway, 2007), 232.

[6] J. North, "The Text's the Thing: Reflections from the Humanities," in *The Two Tasks of the Christian Scholar: Redeeming the Soul, Redeeming the Mind,* ed. W. L. Craig and P. M. Gould (Wheaton, IL: Crossway, 2007), 171.

elements, noting sarcastically that "correct and sober taste may refuse to admit that there can be an interest for *us*—the proud *we* that includes all intelligent living people—in ogres and dragons."[7] In the process of dissecting the poem for minutiae, he believed, they had bled the patient to death on the operating table, completely ignoring the fact that the poem is a story, a narrative that is powerful and worthy of our considerations on the merits of that quality as much if not more so than the linguistic or technical aspects.

The same scolding could perhaps be leveled at how we sometimes treat biblical narrative. It is almost as if we apply 1 Cor 13:11 to the Scriptures themselves: "When I was a child, I spoke like a child, I thought like a child, I reasoned like a child. When I became a man, I put aside childish things." Like *Beowulf*'s critics, we are guilty of parsing and dissecting the Scriptures in ways that can create a sense of embarrassment at the simplicity of the narrative itself, sort of an embarrassment at the childish ways of some passages.

Further, we seem to be shame-faced by the emotions that would come from making a clear connection between our own lives and the stories of the biblical text. I cannot read the description of Abraham's near sacrifice of Isaac without nearly being moved to tears, without thinking of my own son on that altar. What's more, I cannot think, then, of Christ on the cross without seeing it through the eyes of His Father and without thinking of His Sonship through my own eyes relative to my own son. For many of us, emotion is not something to be embraced within the faith; it is too squishy, too subjective. It is in some ways the opposite of intellect. Biblical narrative, however, is very emotional. It calls on us to break out the sackcloth sometimes, to cry tears of joy in other places, and to sigh in awe at God's power in still others. A complete faith is one that includes and balances both emotion and intellect.

In *Blue Like Jazz*, Miller laments how his "Sunday school teachers had turned the Bible narrative into children's fables."[8] His

---

[7] J. R. R. Tolkien, "*Beowulf:* The Monsters and the Critics," in *Interpretations of "Beowulf": A Critical Anthology*, ed. R. D. Fulk (Bloomington: Indiana University Press, 1991), 22.

[8] D. Miller, *Blue Like Jazz: Nonreligious Thoughts on Christian Spirituality* (Nashville: Thomas Nelson, 2003), 30.

complaint is that the great stories of the Scriptures were constantly sanitized and reworked out of what he perceived to be a sense of embarrassment or even shame: "I felt as if Christianity, as a religious system, was a product that kept falling apart, and whoever was selling it would hold the broken parts behind his back trying to divert everybody's attention. The children's story stuff was the thing I felt Christians were holding behind their back."[9]

This impulse to treat the Bible's narratives as simple stories for children, stories that are left behind as one grows older and more intellectually sophisticated, creates in some minds an overly facile approach to theology in particular and to Christianity as a whole. Miller's parting observation about this struggle is pointed: "I couldn't give myself to Christianity because it was a religion for the intellectually naïve. In order to believe Christianity, you either had to reduce enormous theological absurdities into children's stories or ignore them. The entire thing seemed very difficult for my intellect to embrace."[10]

I must admit that I have in many ways rediscovered the literary power of the Bible's narratives in new ways since the birth of my children. My personal devotional readings have always tended to focus on the theologically potent epistles and the poetically masterful Psalms. I have, however, rediscovered the impact that comes from reading the grand narratives of the Old Testament, the implicit stories behind John the Beloved's exhortations in the Johannine Epistles, and the grand story arc of the entirety of Luke's Gospel and the Acts of the Apostles. The Restoration Narrative helps to restore the narrative power of the Scripture itself.

Cultivating a Love for the Christian Intellectual Tradition

I enjoy hearing the stories of people's intellectual pilgrimages: how they became the kinds of thinkers that they are. One of the saddest parts of many of these stories is how often I hear that people were told by well-meaning Christian mentors that they

---

[9] Ibid., 30.
[10] Ibid., 31.

could not be _____ and be a Christian. I have heard this from artists, scientists, musicians, writers, politicians, and many other professions.

This kind of thinking results from the evangelical community's poor handling of the Christian intellectual tradition. In general, most evangelicals have been raised in ignorance of the great gushing stream of thought that is central to the best that has been thought and written over the millennia. For generations, storytellers have been producing narratives that are rooted in the gospel experience, in ways that reflect implicitly the Restoration Narrative.

Growing up, I heard about C. S. Lewis every now and again, and I knew that many "ancient" writers had been Christians on at least a nominal level, but in my mind most everyone in the West had been Christians after Christ's birth, so I never really thought about how there might be an intellectual tradition that was specifically Christian in how it constructed its worldview.

As a literature student, for example, I studied the poetry of T. S. Eliot in many classes; I taught his works for several years at a variety of levels as well. One day when I was doing some background reading, I ran across a stray comment from a scholar that indicated that Eliot had undergone a deep conversion experience when he was 39 or so. The shift in Eliot's poetry was dramatic (see "Ash Wednesday" in particular). The shift in his literary criticism was even more dramatic. I could say the same for the writings of John Updike, who was a deeply religious man. The more I sought to find theologically astute, faithful persons in the literary canon, the more of them I found.[11] In fact, each Sunday when I picked up our hymnals at church, I saw the lions of the English canon: William Cowper, George Herbert, Henry Wadsorth Longfellow, Alfred Lord Tennyson, William Wordsworth, and so many others.

---

[11] I should be clear that I cannot vouch for the complete theological orthodoxy of these writers any more than I can vouch for the complete orthodoxy of all of the members of my church. Within the framework of orthodoxy, there are many areas of disagreement that Christians of genuine faith can find; within the same framework, however, there is more to agree upon that matters eternally. By defining these writers as "Christian," I am reflecting on the ways that these writers have characterized themselves and their work.

Literary critic John North has had a similar experience. He too explored this tradition as he was learning his craft and now notes

> I have discovered that most of the canon of English literature as well as many non-canonical works have been written by self-confessed Christians, men and women using this art form to glorify God in carrying out the two tasks of saving souls and minds. Wonderful that my profession has required me to instruct so many thousands of students in the works of Tennyson, Browning, Shakespeare, Chaucer, Milton, Herrick, the Bronte sisters, Jane Austen, John Ruskin, Charles Dickens, T. S. Eliot, e. e. cummings—all these Christ-confessors.[12]

For a variety of reasons, the Christian elements of these authors and their works is either ignored or is referred to as "quaint" by secularists. Worse yet, the majority of even educated Christians are themselves ignorant of the richness of this tradition.[13]

Mark Twain once observed that there is little difference between those who cannot read and those who chose not to do so. The same logic applies to the Christian intellectual tradition: there is little difference between those who are ignorant of it and those who choose to neglect it intentionally. The net effect is the same: we have lost contact with the great Christian minds of the past. In losing this connection with the past, we have forced ourselves continually to rediscover the lessons learned in former times. Such continuous restarting of an intellectual tradition limits the overall progression of that tradition; nothing can be built on previous thinking.

---

[12] J. North, "The Text's the Thing: Reflections from the Humanities," 162–63.

[13] The Christian intellectual tradition, however, is not really about intellectual hagiography. It is a tradition of principles derived from the Scriptures and from Christian practice. When we shift our observations from the "who" of the tradition to the "what" and the "why," we will be able to see more clearly the abiding principles that undergird both the philosophical foundations and the practical applications of the historical body of work that falls under this category.

Worse yet, this mode of thinking tends to be facile if it is not grounded in the great thinking of the past. As C. S. Lewis once noted,

> This very obvious fact—that each generation is taught by an earlier generation—must be kept very firmly in mind. . . . None can give to another what he does not possess himself. No generation can bequeath to its successor what it has not got. You may frame the syllabus as you please. But when you have planned and reported *ad nauseum*, if we are skeptical we shall teach only skepticism to our pupils, if fools only folly, if vulgar only vulgarity, if saints sanctity, if heroes heroism. . . . Nothing which was not in the teachers can flow from them into the pupils. We shall all admit that a man who knows no Greek himself cannot teach Greek to his form: but it is equally certain that a man whose mind was formed in a period of cynicism and disillusion, cannot teach hope and fortitude."[14]

"Hope and fortitude" are, of course, central to the Christian intellectual tradition, and as one spends time reading the great works written by these writers, the pervasiveness of these qualities is striking.

The power of these Christian narratives is not lost on non-Christian readers either. Some of these readers hold a simple appreciation for the technical achievement of, say, Dante's *Divine Comedy* or Defoe's *Robinson Crusoe*, or even for the handling of the so-called great human themes that may be found in such works. Sometimes, however, there is more that surfaces as a non-Christian approaches a Christian text. I have had many friends who have used classic works of literature as a means of sharing

---

[14] C. S. Lewis, "On the Transmission of Christianity," in *God in the Dock: Essays on Theology and Ethics,* ed. Walter Hooper (Grand Rapids: Eerdmans, 1970), 116.

Christianity with students in foreign countries (especially "closed" nations that are hostile to religion) and even in settings within the West. The powerful foundation of these works is not lost in the shift to such retellings. Truth is powerful, even when it is reflected, mimetic truth.

Even non-Christian narratives can reflect Christian truth, especially when they adapt biblical narratives as source material.[15] As I mentioned in chapter one, the influence of biblical narratives on the broader literary culture is inestimable. I could fill this entire book with explications of similar biblical narratives that find expression in non-Christian works.

Through the towering influence of both Christian writers and biblical narratives themselves, we have at our fingertips massive portions of the world's libraries available to help us explore God's relationship with this world and our relationships with one another.

Before moving on, I should point out that an exploration of the Christian intellectual tradition should not stop with narrative, either. It should embrace the poetry of John Donne, George Herbert, Alfred Lord Tennyson, Gerard Manley Hopkins, T. S. Eliot, and modern poets like Mark Jarman and Li-Young Lee. It should include other art forms like musical compositions from Handel to Dvorak. It should drink deeply from the visual arts, both classical and contemporary, from Dürer to the emerging artists of the Christians in Visual Arts (CIVA) movement. It should recover the original thoughts of scientists like Isaac Newton, Francis Bacon, and so many others. The foundations of Western thought include a great many theologically motivated minds who sought to glorify God in their works. These thinkers continue to shape our culture; other more recent artists seek to join their ranks. The Christian intellectual tradition continues to march on.

---

[15] I call this process "Raiding Jerusalem": just as Augustine encouraged Christians to raid the gold of Egypt (see discussion below), Christians find their gold mined by post-Christian thinkers. Augustine used the Jewish exodus from Egypt for his metaphor; I use the destruction of the first-century temple in Jerusalem as a parallel event: the temple was destroyed and its furnishings provided, at least traditionally, the funds for the building of the Arch of Titus (which includes images of temple objects) and, possibly, the Colosseum. This tradition provides a startling extension of Augustine's original comments.

Significantly, the Christian intellectual tradition does not stop with Christian writers, or even works that adapt biblical narratives. When we extend it to include works that deal with themes that are dear to the faith, issues like temptation, failure, reconciliation, and redemption, then we have readily available the entire libraries of the world to help us to explore God's relationship with this world.

When we expand the Christian intellectual tradition to include works that deal with explicitly Christian themes, then we have the libraries of the world as a whole at our fingertips. *The Aeneid* provides incredible depictions of temptation and failure. The *Popul Vuh* illustrates powerfully the chaos that is left in the wake of great pride. Sometimes even non-Christian writers deal effectively with themes that are specifically central to Christian theological concerns. As North observed, "Even the despairing search of Franz Kafka ("The Hunger Artist," *The Trial*, "Metamorphosis," "The Country Doctor") and Samuel Beckett (*Waiting for Godot, Krapp's Last Tape*) provide parables of our souls' longing for God."[16] Each theme employs elements of the Restoration Narrative, opening up each work for serious theological consideration. T. S. Eliot once observed that "mediocre writers borrow; great writers steal."[17] The greatest writers in the world have stolen the greatest Story ever told, time and time again. Christians should recognize this Story and seize the opportunity presented by this towering influence.

Even in narratives that predate Christianity, Augustine had a specific comment on this kind of "mining" of secular literature for Christian applications. In "On Christian Doctrine" and *Confessions*, he wrote that all truth is truth, no matter where it may be found. Since God is the source of all truth, all truth is God's truth. For Augustine, this opened the doors to reading pagan writings and learning from them. As he noted, the Israelites left Egypt

---

[16] North, "The Text's the Thing," 163.

[17] The actual quotation is "Immature poets imitate; mature poets steal," which has been incorrectly passed down in the form cited. The source is T. S. Eliot, "Philip Massinger," in *The Sacred Wood: Essays on Poetry and Criticism* (1922; reprinted New York: Dover, 1979). Web version at http://www.bartleby.com/200/sw11.html.

behind them but looted its gold for their eventual use in the furnishings of the temple.[18] In the same way, Christians can glean the truth from non-Christians, who have, in fact, borrowed God's truth for their purposes. In this way, Christians are redeeming the truth back to its correct Owner.

When we read narratives that inspire us to honor, duty, or even love, those characteristics are understood most fully in the light of God's self-revelation. The lessons of Daniel and his colleagues in captivity seem to imply that because God had given them "knowledge and understanding in every kind of literature and wisdom" (Dan 1:17), no one else was found to rival their talents. The literature that they studied was pagan through and through, but clearly they applied it in ways that found favor not only with their captors but also with God, for Daniel was used mightily to influence the Babylonian culture. Such was their mission: engaging their context for the sake of God's glory.

Reading Reflectively

Books like E. D. Hirsch Jr.'s *Cultural Literacy: What Every American Needs to Know*[19] are attractive for those who reject what C. S. Lewis called the "chronological snobbery" so epidemic in contemporary intellectual culture: anything old is useless. Such a stance is very modern; the ancients practiced an inverse snobbery: anything new was impertinent. Educated persons should read a variety of resources across a variety of ages.

While there is extraordinary value in calls to return to basics, so to speak, there is a corollary danger that accompanies these invitations to learn about the texts and ideas that have shaped our culture. When we are told that we must learn about them, many people think that this means that we are to master facts and details, not to reflect on the meanings and applications of the works. Such a mindset inadvertently relegates great texts to the past, trivia to

---

[18] Augustine, *Confessions,* trans. F. J. Sheed (Lanham MD: Sheed and Ward, 1944), 113.
[19] E. D. Hirsch Jr., *Cultural Literacy: What Every American Needs to Know* (New York: Vintage, 1988).

be memorized but kept hermetically sealed off from "real life." Worse, such an attitude toward the text is really a softened, more subtle version of the postmodern stances that propose that text holds no meaning, that it is just "words on a page."

The key to appreciating any kind of literature, and narrative in particular, includes the final steps of interpretation: reflection and integration. Memorizing a list of characters in *The Aeneid*, along with a basic plot outline, is worthwhile but is defective without an actual reading of the text and reflection on it. It is akin to the admonition in Jas 1:22 to be doers of the word and not merely hearers.

The ultimate means of learning *from* narrative is the notion of reading reflectively; it involves not simply mastering the facts but rather pondering the ways that the narratives might actually influence our lives.

Until the second half of the twentieth-century, literary studies almost always focused on the ethical applications of narratives. Aristotelian poetics is almost wholly geared toward an affective hermeneutic. The reaction against ethical application, however, is partially rooted in the idea that there can be no authoritative connection between the text and the reader. This resistance toward anything that smacks of authority is one of the reasons that students so readily shun the humanities, which historically have been one of the sources of understanding and ordering life and its ideals. Without those ideals, what's the point? As even secular critic Mark Edmunson has noted, "The test of a book lies in its power to map or transform a life."[20]

Reading Relationally

One of the great values of narrative is its ability to put flesh onto what had previously been only abstraction, which is an

---

[20] M. Edmundson, *Why Read?* (New York: Bloomsbury, 2004), 129. *Why Read?* is an excellent secular apology for reading narrative, reflecting Edmundson's personal longing for a secular version of what has previously been the realm of religious belief: "Literature is, I believe, our best goad toward new beginnings, our best chance for what we might call secular rebirth. However much society at large despises imaginative writing, however much those supposedly committed to preserve and spread literary art may demean it, the fact remains that in literature there abide major hopes for human renovation" (3).

incarnational view of narrative. When I think of a Chinese woman who lived in the third century BC, I have a hard time relating to her. When I find, however, that a poet told the story of her love for a young man and how they had been kept apart by her parents (as is the case of "Chung-Tzu, Please"), then I can begin to relate to that long-dead person.[21] Her world is not my world, but as fellow humans, we share experiences that allow us to connect over the centuries. Art, in this case, not only reflects life; it enhances it by reminding me that I am not alone in my thoughts or feelings.

Further, narrative can provide heretofore unknown experiences. Science fiction is, of course, an extreme version of this. Doris Lessing's *Space Trilogy* takes readers to universes that provide them with a glimpse of how to be more sensitive in this world toward oppression and hurt. Less glamorously, Aldous Huxley's *Brave New World* portrays the pervasiveness of self-slavery in our contemporary culture (and the ease with which people sell themselves into bondage). Travel narratives introduce cultures not previously known. Almost all stories introduce characters and conflicts that the audience can only imagine. In some cases, they are characters and conflicts that the audience may prefer to experience only through storytelling!

Traditionally, a primary way of understanding narrative's relational element is through the lens of loneliness, for stories help us to put our alienation behind us in some way. This is, of course, a valid way of experiencing narrative, and it has been one of the reasons that storytelling is such a powerful and comforting force. Perhaps there is a spiritual truth at work in this, as each of us longs to find a connection with someone else, a genuine friend who anticipates the true Friend that we find ultimately in Christ. Narrative, then, would in part sound out that infamous God-shaped void that each person feels, as Pascal once termed it.

I mention these powers of narrative because of a problem that is persistent among Christians: our ideological and personal isola-

---

[21] "Chung-Tzu, Please," in *The Norton Anthology of World Literature,* vol. A: *Beginnings to A.D. 100,* 2nd ed., trans. S. Owen (New York: W. W. Norton, 2002), 817.

tion. I took a course in evangelism once that required us to share our faith with other persons several times a week. One of my classmates raised his hand and said, "Where do we find these persons? Everyone I know is already a Christian." While most Christians would not like to admit it, most of us do not have close friends who are not believers. This leads to a kind of soft universalism, a subconscious belief that everyone is really saved and that we do not need to share our faith. My students often call this way of thinking the "bubble," which is their way of saying that Christians often create a parallel universe of their own where everyone is a person of faith. Lostness, then, is shocking and, indeed, strange.

The transforming effects of grace make it difficult for us to remember the pain of unforgiven sin. We lose sight of the hopelessness and desperation that accompany a broken relationship with God. We separate ourselves from the sheer anxiety that imbues a fallen world. When we read Thoreau's famous statement that the "mass of men lead lives of quiet desperation,"[22] we have a hard time relating because of the hope that is within us. This is, indeed, where narrative is a necessary tonic for Christians.

Narrative can be startling in its depictions of sin and desperation. Indeed, some narrative is constructed by pagans to satisfy pagan lusts, and it is the wary thinker who wades into such waters without armor aplenty. Having said that, however, reading the hopelessness of, say, Albert Camus's *The Stranger* provides a strong reminder of the hopelessness of a lost world. Such works contain the yawp and cry of a dying world that knows it is damned and seeks solace and satisfaction in things that do not provide ultimate healing. Meursault (*The Stranger*'s main character) projects the voice of the dark night of the soul in which most of the world lives. His thoughts contain the dim memories of the kind of life a Christian lived before submitting to the lordship of Christ, memories which are heavy with regret and a lack of hope. The weight of Meursault's darkness of the soul should move the audience to tears. If it moves Christian readers to shed the same tears for the

---

[22] H. D. Thoreau, *Walden* (1854; repr., New York: Dover, 2001), 7.

lostness of neighbors and other fellow persons, then even Camus has provided godly thoughts to at least one reader.

Ironically, narrative helps us to connect with the lives of our fellow persons through the actions of invented persons. In a fallen world, there is an extent to which anything that even remotely approaches an ideal must be invented. This is particularly true of the human element. Ideal persons, men such as Atticus Finch (*To Kill a Mockingbird*) and Galahad (of the Arthurian legends) and women such as Phoenix Jackson (Eudora Welty's "A Worn Path") and Isabella (Shakespeare's *Measure for Measure*), are heroes indeed, even if they are characters and not "real persons." As Mark Bertrand has observed, "Most of the people we admire, the ones we want to be like, all have one thing in common: *they are made up.*"[23] This artificiality, however, should not be a barrier to our employing such characters to help us to be better persons and to treat others in better ways.

Indeed, reading redemptively means seeing the world with fresh eyes that recognize the lostness that requires redemption and restoration. This is no less true in reading ancient narrative than it is in reading contemporary literature. Narrative moves us to view our shared humanity in ways that can be quite uncomfortable.

Along these same lines, reading redemptively reminds us that we are fallible creatures, subject to temptation and failure. Classical drama sought to warn its culture that if great men could fall, ordinary men likewise should take care to live circumspectly. This is, certainly, a wise sentiment. We live in a culture that enjoys *Schadenfreude*, the vicarious enjoyment derived from beholding the pain and suffering of others, particularly those who are well-off or powerful. We forget, however, that the troubles of other persons are, indeed, the same troubles that each of us will suffer at some point.

This effect is particularly true regarding temptation and failure. Even secular narrative has a strong tendency to derive conflict from the failures of persons to live up to their social contracts with others. Virgil's Dido, indeed, commits suicide because of her treat-

---

[23] M. Bertrand, *(Re)Thinking Worldview: Learning to Think, Live, and Speak in This World* (Wheaton: Crossway, 2007), 166.

ment at the hands of Aeneas. Such depictions parallel the moral exempla from biblical narratives such as those about King David and his sons and daughters. When he succumbs to temptation with Bathsheba, the entire moral order of his family and his kingdom falls into chaos. Witnessing such failures in others as well as the shocking aftereffects in the characters' lives yields a sobering reminder about temptation and sin. The effect is especially important: how much better is it to be reminded about temptation through a character than through our own personal experiences? It is better to read about Aeneas's failures and to heed Virgil's warnings than to live through such failures in our own lives.

The tendency of secular narrative to include frank depictions of immorality, sometimes in terms that affirm its participation, is troubling to many Christian readers. As Darren Middleton has observed, "I have discovered that Christian readers tend to dismiss secular fiction as theologically scandalous, because it promotes ideas that violate the so-called permissible bounds of traditional Christian speculation."[24] Indeed, we walk a tightrope between two scriptural traditions in our engagement with the secular world.

On the one hand, we know that when we are faithful to God's principles, we are able to remain unstained by the world. Christ Himself noted that it is not what comes into our mouths that makes us unclean but rather what proceeds from it (Matt 15:10–12). Also, God's words to Peter in his vision are helpful (Acts 11). Just as Christ came into the world and remained pure, Christians likewise can follow this action by remaining faithful to their God-given calling to glorify Him.

When Paul wrote to the early church about how they should view Scripture, he reminded them that they should look for the authority that it has over their lives in very specific ways. In Rom 15:4, he notes, "For whatever was written in the past was written for our instruction, so that we may have hope through endurance and through the encouragement from the Scriptures we may have hope." He reiterates the instructional purpose of the Scriptures

---

[24] D. J. N. Middleton, *Theology after Reading: Christian Imagination and the Power of Fiction* (Waco: Baylor University Press, 2008), 1–2.

again in 2 Tim 3:16–17: "All Scripture is inspired by God and is profitable for teaching, for rebuking, for correcting, for training in righteousness, so that the man of God may be complete, equipped for every good work." Obviously Paul was declaring a specific value for Scripture, but his observations have been extended to more general writings for generations. A notable example of this is found in Edmund Spenser's *Faerie Queene* in which its opening lines provide an invocation that the verses of the epic poem would help "to fashion a gentleman or noble person in virtuous and gentle discipline."[25] While Spenser alluded to a very convoluted tradition in this comment (including such works as the *Mirror for Magistrates* and Baldassare Castiglione's *The Book of the Courtier*), his view was built on Paul's imperatives.

In this way, then, over the centuries, narrative has served a function of providing Christians with a means of learning, of edification, of correction, and of equipping for good works. This exhortative quality of narrative meshes perfectly with the classical notion of narrative as a warning against pride.

On the other hand, though, Paul urges a focus on righteous thoughts that reflect the mind of Christ. Most notably, in Phil 4:8, Paul urges, "Whatever is true, whatever is honorable, whatever is just, whatever is pure, whatever is lovely, whatever is commendable—if there is any moral excellence and if there is any praise—dwell on these things." How much praiseworthy content may be found in reading about the sexual escapades of Jove, for example, in Ovid's *Metamorphoses*? What, then, is a Christian reader to do with such narratives?

A middle ground between both traditions allows faithfulness through the engagement of our world for the gospel. If we isolate ourselves from ungodly persons and if we refuse to engage ungodly ideas and behaviors, then we are violating our calling to evangelize our fallen world. If we fill our minds with unfruitful ruminations, including those from narratives that are ungodly,

---

[25] E. Spenser, "A Letter of the Authors [to Walter Raleigh]," in *The Faerie Queene,* ed. A. C. Hamilton (New York: Longman, 1977), 737; spelling regularized.

to the exclusion of those that are edifying, then we have accomplished the same, only in reverse. Paul's admonition in Phil 4:8, to "dwell on these things," means to "ponder" or "constantly consider" these things, not simply "do not encounter the opposite." In order to communicate the gospel to a dark world, we need to encounter darkness in its fullest effect, in the lives of persons who do not know Christ, and to communicate with such persons, in ways that are effective and redemptive. One of these ways is through a careful, discerning examination of the broad expanse of human narrative.

This point of view asserts the importance of active reading, of considering the readings at hand in light of a person's own place of understanding. The proper term here is "discernment." Every person has a sense of his or her own strengths and weaknesses. Once again, the notion of the full armor of the gospel is helpful here, that we do not wade into frays without carefully considering the challenges that lie ahead or without relying on God's faithfulness to guide and protect us. I also think, however, that we need to consider that the challenges that face some persons do not face others. Corrie ten Boom, in *The Hiding Place,* told a story about how as a young child, she had asked her father a question about sex. Without answering her, he asked her to bring to him his valise. She could not lift it because it was too heavy: "Some knowledge is too heavy for children. When you are older and stronger you can bear it. For now you must trust me to carry it for you."[26] Discernment is hard work and calls for patience, but a lack of willingness to put in the hard work of exercising it can lead to a withdrawal from the world that can prevent serious engagement with it for the sake of the gospel.

A teacher once discussed a short story with her college-aged students. The story had a small amount of coarse language in it, and a student confronted her in front of the class, stating that he would refuse to read any stories that were not explicitly Christian. He said something like, "I don't use language like that, and I don't

---

[26] C. ten Boom, *The Hiding Place* (New York: Bantam, 1971), 26–27.

associate with persons who use language like that. I will not sully myself with unchristian thoughts or ideas."

The teacher gently asked the student what his major was.

"Missions," he replied, puffing out his chest a bit. "I'm going to be a missionary."

She said, "How can you be a missionary if you don't associate with persons who use ungodly language and who think ungodly thoughts? Unless you are going to be a missionary to your grandma's Sunday school class, you had better start to learn how to speak French to a Frenchman. That doesn't mean that you are learning to use coarse language, but rather that you are learning to communicate with a person who does."

Narrative is one of the means that we have, that God has provided for us, to do just that. Discerning reading eschews titillation; it understands lostness. Redemptive reading seeks to find ways to articulate the remedy for such despair. If Christians are so fragile in their faith that they are afraid that simple contact with an idea will destroy their faith, then there is a spiritual issue at the heart of the problem. This is why Paul wrote about the notion of milk / baby Christians (1 Cor 3:1–3). Sometimes the problem is not with the narrative but rather with the reader; I could teach passages out of the Bible in ways that would be offensive. The problem, however, would not be with the text but rather that I had handled it in a way that lacked understanding or even integrity. The same is true with some narrative that is treated in ways that are shallow or incomplete.

A view that Christians should avoid all contact with secular narratives is inconsistent with the biblical witness. Perhaps the best example of this is in Acts 17, the famous passage describing Paul's address on Mars Hill. Paul's knowledge of classical literature allowed him to communicate clearly and directly with a culture that was not his own. Note, in fact, that one of the allusions he makes may be to Ovid, whose aforementioned *Metamorphoses* is filled with pagan immorality, which means that Paul himself knew of the work. His knowledge of biblical and secular narratives allowed him to connect the two worlds in a way that confronted the attendees of the Areopagus with the truth of God's revelation of Himself in Scripture. The direct result of this linkage of pagan and biblical thought was that persons who had not previously understood God now began a relationship with Him.

We are to share our faith fearlessly but also in a way that is comely. When visiting other countries, we always try to read some of their national literature so that we can at least hold a conversation about the major writers of the culture. Being widely read does not find usefulness in international travel alone, however, for our world is a global village.

On a flight to a conference in Texas, I struck up a conversation with a seat-mate who happened to be a businessman from India. When he found out that I am a literature professor, he asked what courses I teach and who my favorite writers are. I mentioned that I teach world literature with some frequency and asked if he had ever read *The Rāmāyana* (which would be akin to asking an American if he had ever read anything about Abraham Lincoln). He was obviously tickled to hear that I had read it, and we started talking about the story.

At one point, I asked him about the story's emphasis on karma, the notion that the universe requires that we balance out our sins or errors with good works and obedience to the divine principle (dharma). I asked him what he thought about the notion that Rāma had suffered in order to teach humankind that suffering is redemptive. He gleefully spoke to the issue, explaining that his culture had seen the value of suffering, that it helped to move life along toward its next levels (through reincarnation). When he was done, I asked him if this meant that every person had to bear the burden of their own release from the bondage of their failures. He affirmed this and added, "This is why it takes many lifetimes to achieve enlightenment."

He smiled and said, "Of course, Rāma is just like Jesus of the Christian faith. Jesus likewise taught us that suffering was redemptive." I returned his smile but added, "Actually, Jesus did something different: He didn't suffer in order to teach us how to suffer. He suffered in our places. He paid the cost for our failures so that we don't have to in the eternal sense. That's what Christianity calls 'grace.'"

This point caused him to think. After all, the possibility that grace might trump karma every time is one of the crucial differences between the two faith systems. Suddenly, I understood Paul's speech on Mars Hill in a new light. I saw how the Restoration Narrative's emphasis on restoring that which has been thrown off balance might speak to the heart of someone who had not yet come to a full appreciation of special revelation. I have no idea what happened to that businessman, but God enabled me to communicate the gospel to him in a way that began with the themes of the literary narratives of his homeland.

8

Writing
Redemptively

Abraham took the wood for the burnt
offering and laid it on his son
Isaac. In his hand he took the fire
and the sacrificial knife, and the
two of them walked on together.

—Gen 22:6

The world is charged with the
grandeur of God. / It will flame
out, like shining from shook foil.

—Gerard Manley Hopkins,
"God's Grandeur," lines 1-2.[1]

---

[1] G. M. Hopkins, "God's Grandeur," in *The Norton Anthology of English Literature: The Major Authors,* 6th ed., ed. M. H. Abrams (New York: W. W. Norton, 1996), 2127–28.

I n the West, the idea of telling a "new" story is actually a fairly recent development. Historically, claiming to tell a new story was considered to be almost hubristically presumptive—that the storyteller was equating his skill at spinning a yarn with the greats of the past. Why listen to "Billy Joe's story of a hunting trip" when you could listen to Homer's tale of Troy? For Billy Joe to claim narrative equality to Homer meant that Billy Joe had an ego problem.

"Make it old" was the motto: retell an old tale, set it in the past, and show the audience how the greats of the former ages learned their lessons. In the opening of the famous Middle English poem "Gawain and the Green Knight," the poet includes the simple phrase "as I heard it once in the hall" as evidence that he was telling an old tale. It was not until 1935 that poet-critic Ezra Pound could declare "make it new" in a collection of essays (though in all fairness, he was updating Confucius to some extent), a view that piggybacked on the emerging chronological snobbery of the culture at that point in history.

In the great classics of Greek drama, the presumption was that the audience knew the story's basic plot and even the ending. The skill of the playwright was in the shaping of the story, not in its root creation. This approach to storytelling has many advantages, in that characters can be developed over time and even across narrators. The "new" storytellers add vigor to the narrative, expanding it and grafting in new details. Nineteenth-century scholars of folklore called this the *lieder Theorie*, that minstrels shaped narratives over time, each adding his own stamp to the overall arc of the story.

Similarly, I once heard a very successful popular songwriter say that writing a hit pop song pushed him in one of two directions: either he tried to write a Beatles song, or he tried to write a hymn. Quickly, he played the basic chords of several of his most popular compositions, and it was amazing how true his observation was. What he meant was that he was tapping into a powerful format of familiar phrasing, into something that was powerful, even mythic.

For the Greeks, a myth was not a false tale; a myth was a powerful story, rooted in the truth of the human experience, which gave meaning and substance to the culture. For them, a myth was a conduit for awesome power, for the storyteller was stepping into the very stream of history itself and channeling the power of that stream through the narrative. Myth connected the past with the present, adding the storyteller's voice to that of history in a way that the audience might drink deeply from the well of history's lessons. Myths were the gold from which the bards and sages wrought their treasuries of tales. They had the power to advise, to chasten, to warn, and to admonish the highest of leaders and the lowliest of slaves.

For Christians who desire to write, the call to read broadly is an absolute necessity, for writing is, in many ways, the process of digesting and synthesizing not only the thoughts and experiences of a writer's own life, but the writer's intellectual wanderings as well.

The creative writing program in which I teach takes this observation quite seriously, as we require writing majors to take a large number of literature courses on the way to producing their senior capstone portfolio of works. This breadth of literary knowledge helps our students to understand the foundational concepts into which they are tapping with their own work. In many ways, this reflects something of a classical approach to writing, in which students are encouraged to imitate other writers before trying to create their own works out of whole cloth.

A review of almost all successful writers' lives will reveal that their reading habits are uniformly compendious. One of the most interesting parts of author interviews is the discussion of their favorite books and writing heroes. Even more interesting is the force that resistance to previous traditions has produced; humans are shaped as much by influences with which they agree as they are by concepts with which they disagree.

As I teach undergraduate writing students, I occasionally encounter a youthful boast about wanting to write but hating to read. I always smirk at this and ask, "Okay, so how does that business model work? You want to be a writer, but you don't read or purchase books written by other writers. I believe that you aren't entitled to be a published writer until you are a participating member of the writing community, and that starts with both purchasing and reading books in your chosen genre." That usually gets their attention. In fact, in my introductory writing classes, I require my students to purchase a specific dollar amount of contemporary books, usually poetry or fiction.

Roman writer Horace rather famously called good literature "sweetness and light." It was sweet in that it entertained, and it was light in that it illuminated the mind of the reader. The combination of pleasure and enlightenment made literature a powerful tool for shaping a person's thoughts and attitudes. In fact, the bee often symbolized literature, for it produced the honeycomb. The honey from the comb brought sweetness, and the comb itself could be melted to produce candle wax.

This tension between sweetness and light has driven the study of literature for centuries, in that there is always a tendency for writers to veer into one without the other. Certainly, there are plenty of light-weight stories, fluffy light-hearted entertainment that contains little substance. Much of the entertainment media that fill our airways currently falls into this category, as does much of popular fiction. On the other hand, there are many heavy-handed tomes that heap facts and opinions on the reader without much in the way of entertainment or engagement.

These twin challenges are important in the consideration of the mission of writing redemptively: how do we avoid writing fluff and at the same time avoid easy didacticism? The answer, I believe, comes from remembering *whose* story we are telling in the first place. C. S. Lewis once observed, "What we want is not more little books about Christianity, but more little books by Christians on other subjects—with their Christianity *latent*."[2] He was calling for Christians to escape the "ghetto" of the faith com-

---

[2] C. S. Lewis, "On the Transmission of Christianity," in *God in the Dock: Essays on Theology and Ethics,* ed. Walter Hooper (Grand Rapids: Eerdmans, 1970), 93.

munity by engaging the broader world with excellence and truth. For those whose specific calling, whose mission in life is to connect with larger cultures through the written word, the generation of fresh literary works is a high calling, indeed, when it is carried out for its intended purpose: the praise of God.

Writer as Praise-Giver: Whose Story Shall We Tell?

F. Scott Fitzgerald's *The Great Gatsby* is among my favorite novels, precisely because I have a personal connection with its story. I had read it several times in my education, but when I landed my first high school teaching position right after graduate school, I had to teach it to eleventh graders, so I opened it afresh to prepare. I read it at my new home, a rented guest cottage on a multi-millionaire Polish duke's estate in Virginia. It was a waterfront estate that was once a part of the property of George Washington's ancestors. The river was a branch of the Chesapeake Bay, and on late summer evenings, I could stand on the pier and watch the parties of the wealthy underway up the shore. There were even flickering green lights at the ends of many of the piers, just like those in the harbor between the Eggs in *Gatsby*. At some point in my reading, I realized that I was Nick Carraway, the rather penniless observer of the wealthy. I had a view but no standing. I learned their ways, but I knew that I would unlikely have the resources actually to participate as a full-fledged member of that society. I grew to adore the novel precisely because I felt as though I were a character in it.

This personal connection to narrative is foundational to what I think should be a powerful consideration in how Christian authors approach their work. Most writers are compelled overwhelmingly to tell not just any story but, in many cases, a thinly veiled version of *their* story. I know that I draw heavily on my own experiences as I write: people I have known, things I have done, stories I have heard, and so forth. I know that I must drive my parents crazy as they recognize these things in my writing, even as they wonder if some of the harsher parts of the narratives are really about me. I wrote a story about suicide once that included some very personal stories from my own experience that influenced the protagonist, even though I have never personally struggled with that issue. I have, however, had several friends who have, so the protagonist is really a mixture of my life and theirs.

I grew up in churches that valued personal testimony. I seem to remember that Wednesday evening prayer meetings were especially prone to include testimonies as a part of the services. Someone would stand up and give thanks to God for rescuing him from alcohol or drugs or some other ill, and the congregation would say "amen" to God's power in that event.

Sometimes the occasion was that of a conversion experience (often at the end of a Sunday service). Sometimes the occasion was that of the miraculous (often right before the offering or the special music). Sometimes the occasion was that of a personal failure that had been rectified (almost always on Wednesday night prayer meetings). I heard stories of drug abuse, alcoholism, whoremongering (I had no idea what it was, but it sounded utterly disgraceful), and prodigality. Prime-time television had nothing on our congregation, at least in my sheltered eyes.

As anyone who has been a part of these services knows, however, there is a tendency for testimonies to turn from being stories about God to stories about the self. That the word "I" becomes sprinkled into the narrative to the exclusion of "He" marks a dramatic shift in what the point of the story actually is. Appropriate testimonies tend to move from "I" and "me" to "God" and "He."

This, however, reflects the purpose of the writer's mission: finding ways to communicate God's glory. The purpose of a genuine testimony is that of declaring praise to God for His role in one's life. The focus is supposed to be on God, rather than on the sinner or the struggler or the storyteller. Good testimonies, indeed the most powerful ones, are those that directly reflect God's redemptive, grace-filled power rather than the obscuring egocentrism of the person. Ironically, I sense that the tearful testimonies that made me feel the most awkward were likely the ones that conveyed the strongest sense of God's goodness and a personal sense of humility before God.

For Christian writers, the lessons taught by the ancients are instructive, as they sought to tap into the power of the old stories. For Christians, the glorification of God provides access to a power that is dynamic indeed. The Restoration Narrative provides a framework that can help to guide our storytelling in ways that are faithful to God's own Story. Our stories do not have to be explicitly "Christian" (which tends to mean "preachy") in order to be Christian; we can convey the truth as understood in the light of God's wisdom through poetry, fiction, and creative nonfiction in ways that are sweet to the palate of our audiences.

What Is the Christian Distinctive?

I had never really thought much about writing redemptively or "Christianly" before I arrived at Union University, and I certainly had never thought about how to teach creative writing in a way that is distinctively Christian. Over the past few years, though, I have pondered this notion at length. It is the pressing question of my pedagogy and my scholarship: what unique element(s) of the Christian faith can inform my intellectual life and work?

Of course, the primary distinctive of Christianity is the Christ of the Bible and the gospel underpinnings that I have outlined elsewhere in this book. Certainly, there is much overlap among the major religions in the world, including basic moral frameworks and the concepts of sin and forgiveness. The uniqueness of Christianity, though, is in many ways the absolute inability of humankind to achieve their own salvation and the voluntary reconciliation / atonement that was achieved by Christ during His ministry on earth. Hinduism's great epic, *The Rāmāyana*, provides a contrasting example of the Christian notion of salvation. Its main character, Rāma, is an incarnation of Vishnu who teaches humankind to suffer in pursuit of nirvana, but Vishnu does not suffer in the stead of humankind. He suffers rather as an example to humankind. Christ, of course, suffers in the place of humankind, allowing us to rely on His labors to effect our reconciliation with the divine.

The Rāmāyana, however, still follows the Restoration Narrative framework, even as it substitutes an incorrect means of restoration. It still retains the power of the meta-narrative to which it corresponds. The power of the redemptive meta-narrative is, indeed, the source of power for Christians who would write effective literary narratives. Perhaps a biblical model would be helpful.

As I mentioned in chapter five, Genesis 22 follows the basic outline of the Restoration Narrative: the beloved child is born to great rejoicing of, and not a little bit of testifying to, God's incredible movement in the lives of Abraham and Sarah. The aged couple enters into an idyllic time of joy; indeed, this is the golden age of their golden years, as they watch the young man grow. The commandment to sacrifice the son breaks this perfection, casting Abraham into a horrible time of testing, where he surely must doubt God's purpose. The imperfection reaches a climax in the moment when Isaac is bound on the altar and Abraham is about to plunge the knife into his chest. At that moment, the divine voice returns and intervenes, breaking the imperfection and providing a substitutionary sacrifice, a ram. The narrative tension is released, and the golden age is not only restored but also elevated to a previously underestimated state.

While the story certainly is foundational to Judaism, as it underscores the singular covenant between God and Abraham, the hindsight of Christianity amplifies this original context through the lens of Christ's substitutionary atonement. The imperfection is relieved via Abraham's faithful actions, but his faith is undergirded and put into effect not through his sacrifice of Isaac but through his willingness to sacrifice him: his will is wholly reliant on God's leading and is submissive to His will. The restoration, though, is effected by the substitution of the ram for the son, which Abraham joyfully offers as a sacrifice in lieu of his son. For Christian interpreters, this substitution is an emotional foreshadowing of how God the Father will allow His Son to be sacrificed on behalf of humankind, as John 3:16 puts it, "that everyone who believes in Him will not perish but have eternal life." For Christians, the complete glory of the story is not found until we realize that this is, in fact, a template for the gospel narrative of the New Testament.

Genesis 22:6 contains a heartbreaking undertone: "Abraham took the wood for the burnt offering and laid it on his son Isaac. In his hand he took the fire and the sacrificial knife, and the two of them walked on together." In Abraham's story, the fire was a small smoldering set of embers carried in a leather pouch that could be used to start a fire, in this case the flames that would consume the sacrifice. The knife was probably an obsidian blade that would be used to slash the boy's throat, just before the fire was kindled into a blazing sacrifice.

Since I am a literary critic, I trade on symbolism, and I find the symbolism of these two items to be instructive to writers who wish to imbue their work with specifically Christian elements that are not simply didactic.

In the fire, I see a power that is handed down from generation to generation, for fire was an important commodity for nomadic persons like Abraham. Embers were to be cared for and maintained at all costs. When fire went out, it could be restarted from scratch with some difficulty, but usually it was easier to borrow some from neighbors, who would hand it over as a part of the hospitality that their culture prized. Sharing in the fire was an act of joining together in the great stream of communal life. Writing redemptively involves the same kind of commitment, for it steps into the gushing stream of the Christian intellectual tradition, borrowing the fires of Augustine, Dante, Chaucer, Shakespeare, Bunyan, Milton, Thackery, Chesterton, Eliot, Tolkien, and Lewis in an effort to bring glory to God without fear. Writing redemptively shares in the communal flames that have been passed down by these brilliant thinkers and artists.

Further, in the fire we see the power that is transferred from one storyteller to the next. The purest form of this power is that of the Restoration Narrative, which taps directly into the ultimate story of God Himself. The Greek word for "fire," *pur*, reminds us of the purification that fire provides metals, removing the dross from the element; there is a responsibility that Christian writers bear to maintain a purity that is defined by biblical authority and Christian traditions. Christian writers must take upon themselves an effort to remove the dross from their own representations of Truth. What I mean is that there are theological boundaries beyond which a Christian writer should not trespass. One of the most common dangers that Christian writers entertain is the temptation to recast the theological concepts according to their own understandings.

Theological concepts do not have to be heavy-handed attempts to give fictive faces to systematic, rational approaches to the faith. They do, however, have to be "Christian" in order to be rightly thought of as "Christian." They should reside somewhere within the generous boundaries of basic, historical orthodoxy. Christian writers should be students of both human experience and fundamental theological discourse.

The other tool is the knife, which I take as a symbol for the way that the narrative can cut deeply to the core of our being. This is a knife that is jagged, one that does not allow for simple, neat answers. It is a dramatic tool for conveying truth through the messiness of human experience.

For some reason, an urge exists that sanitizes the suffering necessary for the atonement. Somehow, our imaginations cannot fully appreciate the stark punishment that He undertook in order to effect our redemption. We often make it almost yawningly passive, as though it happened in the blink of an eye, with minimal blood and minimal pain. Such a view of the atonement creates in us a sense that the sacrifice really was not that great, that our sins were not as bloody as they really were (and are), and that the imbalance that Christ sought to restore was not really all that tenuous.

The sacrifice of Abraham's ram was bloody business, however. The throat was slashed. Blood was spilt. Fire was burned. Christ's sacrifice was no less bloody. For writers, there is a picture of the reality of the conflict about which we write. The chasm between God and humanity, the chasm between humans, and the chaos that engulfed our world in the wake of the fall are great indeed, and ones that deserve to be told accurately, blood and all.

Christians who employ the knife in their writing will be unafraid, then, to depict the kind of fallenness that demands redemption, the kind of imbalance that craves restoration. When we write stories that are happy, with little conflict or inference about sin, then we are creating portraits of the world that perpetuate a sort of "soft universalism," the idea that no one is truly lost but rather that all are really saved. Such a view does not comport with the broad view of Scripture or tradition.

Moreover, a lack of conflict or a shallow imbalance does not comport with the experiences of the world outside of the faith. It is, in the most literal sense, unrealistic. If it is unrealistic, then it is irrelevant.

Perhaps an example would be helpful to illustrate how the fire and the knife are both necessary to fully functioning Christian narrative. William Paul Young's blockbuster novel, *The Shack,* is a bestseller in both Christian and secular book charts.[3] Its popularity resulted directly from its realistic portrayal of one man's tremendous grief. This popularity, however, has been matched by the scathing criticism it has received from some quarters of the faith community.

The novel tells the story of Mack, a man who has endured horrible loss. The opening pages are gut punches, brutally assaulting the emotions of the reader. Anyone who is a parent will find

---

[3] W. P. Young, *The Shack* (Los Angeles: Windblown Media, 2007) attempts to be a *Pilgrim's Progress* for its day, so perhaps I should comment a bit on John Bunyan's classic work. *Pilgrim's Progress* is an extended allegory, produced during an era when allegory was a dominant genre in the Western tradition. As a genre, readers and authors alike knew how to read the shorthand conventions that the work expressed. *Pilgrim's Progress* is not, rightly understood, character-driven in the way that I mean, precisely because the readers of the seventeenth century did not read it as literary fiction but rather as allegory, which attempts to bring abstractions into a kind of concrete story. Readers of Bunyan's day, however, expected it to be about "ideas," as an alternative hybrid of expository prose and narrative. No reader contemporary to Bunyan would have said, "It's only fiction; what's the big deal?" In the same way, no reader of Young should repeat that shrugging question; the propositions espoused by Young deserve to be scrutinized.

particular empathy with Mack's horrific experiences. After a brief time of mourning, Mack is given a vision (or a visitation) of God, "Papa," in the form of an African-American woman. The rest of the Trinity is a part of this experience as well (Jesus is a Mediterranean carpenter, and the Holy Spirit is an Asian woman), each revealing a portion of God's nature, as envisioned by Young.

Originally self-published, *The Shack* topped the *New York Times'* fiction list for some time, selling in excess of one million copies. Fans found its raw emotions and emphasis on God's ability to empathize with humans deeply attractive. Critics found its facile depictions of the Trinity heretical.

Young produced a narrative that understands the power of the knife. His descriptions slash broadly and deeply, leaving wounds that expose the reader's heart and emotions to the raw, cold reality of a fallen world. The novel is brutal in its depictions of sin and the conflicts that overwhelm us: the random nature of the universe, our own broken relationships, and our own difficulties in understanding the ways of God. I have read very little "Christian" fiction that packs the level of power present in *The Shack*. The story cries out for restoration of peace. Mack is an Everyman, in search of the kind of *shalom* that only God can produce this side of eternity. This longing for God is part of what resonated with so many readers.

On the other hand, Young's story fails to maintain the purity of the fire. Trinitarian theology is hard enough to grasp using traditional formats, but moving into symbolic language like fiction is a slippery slope indeed. When he succumbed to modalism (the idea that the three Persons of the Trinity are distinct and do not overlap) in some places of the text, he crossed into the realm of heresy. Worse, perhaps, is the novel's cavalier dismissal of theology as a worthwhile pursuit. The plain pursuit of emotion to the exclusion of rationality is clearly outside the boundaries of biblical injunction and Christian tradition.

Simply stated, the methodology of *The Shack* is a tremendous example of the proper use of the knife, but the application of its content reveals that Young had failed to maintain the purity of the fire. I should, however, be bold in my reminder that orthodoxy is tricky business. No less than John Milton (in *Paradise Lost*) and C. S. Lewis (in *The Last Battle*) have faced criticism that they were promulgating heresy in their works. I think that a hermeneutics of optimism should also include a level of mercy and grace. While writers should strive to maintain orthodoxy, those who are more theologically astute should practice a criticism of humility so long as the works do not violate the sacrosanct principles of the Restoration Narrative, the reality of sin, the truth of the resurrection, and the exclusivity of Christ's redemptive ministry. I am not saying that we need to give a free pass to theological failings within narrative, but rather that we need to be gentle toward one another, even as we point out any shortcomings.

The same gentleness is needed in the other direction. When writers employ the purity of the fire but forget to utilize the power of the knife by failing to include the very *need* for redemption, then this omission veers into heresy as well, by failing to uphold the reality of sin. Once again, I have heard critics of shallow depictions of conflict be brutal in their appraisals of such works. Neither aesthetic nor theological snobbery is acceptable when it expresses itself with bare knuckles. The spirit of Christ is one of mercy, even as it is one of exhortation and admonishment.

A final word about the knife: a call to produce narrative that is cutting and deeply conflicted is not a call to produce crassness. The current push to generate scenes and dialogue that are "gritty and realistic" often results in puerile, offensive material that does not enlighten. I often ask my students if their purpose is to shock or to inform. Do they wish to spend their artistic liberties in the former when they could instead concentrate on the latter? The imagination is a powerful tool of persuasion, and leaving some things to its devices creates much stronger narrative. Sometimes it is better to allude to events than to depict them. At other times, it is better to create rules for oneself and find ways to write around them than simply to abandon good taste entirely. Writers have communicated powerful themes for centuries without the extensive use of four-letter words and graphic depictions of sinfulness.

Christian writers, in particular, have a higher standard, for they carry upon themselves the name of Christ. As we deal with realistic issues, we need to take care not to lose significant portions of our audience along the way.

The Fertile Ground between the Fire and the Knife

If Christian writers face twin ditches in their pursuit of producing truthful narrative, then the ground between the ditches is fertile soil, indeed. Perhaps a better image would be that Christian writers face twin furrows that run alongside a narrow ribbon of raised soil into which they may plant their stories. The power of the fire, restrained by the knife's edges, creates a final opportunity for writers who are seeking to communicate truth through fiction in particular: character-driven stories.

In expository writing, as in essays, a thesis statement dominates the author's approach to the writing medium. That single controlling idea drives the wording, the selection of anecdotes, and ultimately even the choice of the intended audience.

Many years ago I was teaching expository writing at a community college in New Orleans. In that course we emphasized the five-paragraph theme that is common in these kinds of courses, where an introduction, three body paragraphs, and a conclusion form the basic structure of the essay.

One student in that class was a preacher, and one day he exclaimed, "This is just like a sermon: find your passage, figure out your primary theme, select three points to illustrate your theme, and have a good conclusion to tie it all together." That sermon format, what used to be called "three points and a poem," shares a similar source to the five-paragraph theme because both attempt to convey information in a way that is both effective and streamlined.

A good sermon, like a good essay, can follow the arc of the Restoration Narrative; likewise a good sermon should adhere to biblical orthodoxy. Sermons, however, emphasize the speaker as the voice of the message. This reflects the deep roots of Christian sermons as testimonies. In testimonies, even in Peter's sermon in Acts 2 that outlines God's movement through the history of a people, the speakers tell the audience about how God has moved in their lives.

Narrative attempts something entirely different. Good storytelling, of course, has a point that it seeks to communicate, a connection between the mind of the author and the minds of the readers. In fact, great narrative always has multiple layers of complexity that communicate within the story. The narrator's voice, however, is not the central emphasis of literary narrative. The characters themselves are the primary means of communicating the connection between author and readers.

In teaching creative writing, I find that students constantly fight against allowing their characters to be the primary means of communicating. In one of my mentoring sessions with a young writer, I noted that he seemed unable to match his work with the ideals that he held out for himself. His products were always didactic and preachy in the worst way. In fact, in conversations with him, I found him to be the same way—constantly haranguing about what was on his mind.

I gently chided him, "Look, you keep saying that you want to communicate truth in your writings. What's happening, though, is that you keep screaming for attention in the way that you construct everything. You aren't writing about truth, you are writing about yourself."

He looked confused.

"Well, aren't I supposed to write about myself and my ideas?" he protested.

"Yes, but in a way that connects with the reader. You keep turning into the crazy guy who's standing on the street corner screaming at everyone. If you've ever seen that happen in a city, you know that the reaction that 98 percent of the people have is to hurry on their ways and get out of earshot. There's no communication happening, only one-directional shouting. You have to find a way to get out of the way and connect with your audience. If you are writing fiction, you need to use your characters to communicate your ideas."

I could tell that he was flummoxed by this advice.

"But I'm the one with something to say, and I've got a lot of things that I want to say. My head is bursting with ideas, in fact. My characters are only props that I use to decorate my thinking."

I interrupted, "And that's the problem. You think you are communicating truth, but in fact you are only acting as a selfish tyrant who is ruling the universe of your writing. You have set yourself up as the main point. Get down off your self-centered pedestal, and let the truth be the truth. And let your characters communicate the truth."

This story, in a nutshell, illustrates a final failing of much Christian fiction: it devolves into sermonizing. The antidote to sermonizing is the employment of character-driven narratives, carefully guided by an author who seeks to tell God's Story.

In my thinking, the best example of a Christian writer who accomplishes character-driven fiction is Flannery O'Connor, who used almost surreal situations to communicate biblical truth. O'Connor used improbable characters to reveal theological truth. In "A Good Man Is Hard to Find," for example, O'Connor used horrifying violence to communicate the fallenness of the world. In The Misfit, we find human depravity in its rawest form. The story did not end in pure restoration, but it hints at it unequivocally through a central conversation between the grandmother and The Misfit. The result of this conversation was a longing on the part of the audience to see restoration effected through the imposition of justice in such a raw world.

O'Connor's work was totally character-driven. While the main characters certainly incorporate stereotypical elements, they are the primary agents of the story's action. The narrator does not provide the readers with glossy theologizing or preachy interpretation of the story's events. O'Connor's work is, for the most part, theologically orthodox and fairly sophisticated; the conflicts she depicted through her characters are fully orthodox as well in that they reflect accurately a fallen world in need of redemption.

Her narratives include theology that is sparked by the interactions between the characters, which spread into the very minds of the readers.

Perhaps the ultimate irony of character-driven stories is that they play up to the egotism of the audience. The reason that character-driven fiction is of primary importance is very simple: readers do not connect with omniscient, authoritative narrators. Readers connect with characters. If I were to ask a group of people to name their favorite literary characters, I would get a variety of responses. If I asked the same group to name their favorite literary narrators, I would garner a variety of confused looks.

The books that speak to readers most clearly are those that find a strong connection between a main character and the individual readers. In many ways there is a humorous mindset at work with readers: they want to read stories about interesting, exciting, and unique characters who remind them of themselves. Readers empathize with such a character precisely because they are able to see elements of themselves in the characters.

Writing Relationally

By emphasizing the character element of narrative, I am emphasizing the human element of storytelling. While the primary purpose of Christian narrative is that of glorifying God, the application of that overriding purpose is the communication of that glory to other persons. Sharply constructed characters, working within the Restoration Narrative, allow this to happen powerfully.

I have mentioned already the author's love for his characters and the hermeneutic of love that has been proposed by Alan Jacobs. I would like to extend those comments in a new direction. Christian writers should be motivated by a similar love for the audience.

Most writers have a love-hate relationship with audiences. There is frustration when readers fail to discern something that the author has strived to communicate, but there is an equal joy in hearing that one's narratives have been well received or appreciated. I can say with all honesty that in the next world every writer longs to hear Matt 25:21's "Well done, good and faithful slave!," but in this world we long to hear, "I really appreciated your last piece. It really spoke to me."

When I discussed reading redemptively, I mentioned that there is an ethical component to the process of reading. As Mark Edmundson claimed, "The test of a book lies in its power to map or transform a life. . . . The question we would ultimately ask of any work of art is this: Can you live it?"[4] The origin of this burden is not within the reader, however; it is within the writer.

The calling of a Christian writer is the same as the calling of all believers: communicating the truth of God and His love to others. The power of the Restoration Narrative gives us a mode of expression. Our own passions and experiences give us the materials necessary for customizing our message. The final piece of the puzzle is that of cultivating a love for the audience.

The New Testament underscores the importance of love toward one another. This imperative should drive everything that we do, including the way that we generate narrative. First John 3:23 is a clarion call to express our every thought and deed in terms of love: "Now this is His command: that we believe in the name of His Son Jesus Christ, and love one another as He commanded us." An ethic of writing in love means that we do not try to trick our audiences for an empty purpose. We do not perpetuate the myths of meaninglessness and hopelessness. We do not promulgate theological error. We do not imply that the fall has never occurred.

I heard a colleague at another university sneer that Christianity was irrelevant to our contemporary culture because it had nothing to offer. I hear in those words a condemnation not of the faith but of those who practice the faith in the context of the arts. In particular, I hear a critique of the tendency of Christians to create micro-ghettos of intellectual pursuit. We produce tepid works that underwhelm secularists with their sophistication or even their subject matter. Sadly, this is particularly true with evangelicals. Russell D. Moore has stated that Anglo-Catholics are known for

---

[4] M. Edmundson, *Why Read?* (New York: Bloomsbury, 2004), 129.

works like *Lord of the Rings* and *Wise Blood* and films like *The Passion of the Christ* while evangelicals are known for producing Christian romance novels, the Left Behind series, and videos of the Veggie-tales. The latter speak primarily to the choir, so to speak, while the former challenge even the most secular of audiences, confronting them with depictions of God's Story.

I would challenge anyone who believes that Christianity has little to offer a post-religious culture to consider two passages: "Therefore, just as sin entered the world through one man, and death through sin, in this way death spread to all men, because all sinned" (Rom 5:12) and "Pure and undefiled religion before our God and Father is this: to look after orphans and widows in their distress and to keep oneself unstained by the world" (Jas 1:27). Those two passages create the context for writing about death, brokenness, loss, failure, justice, hope, peace, and grace.

I am mindful of what is often called the shortest complete story in English, supposedly written by Ernest Hemingway. It is only six words long: "For sale: baby shoes, never worn." That simplest of narratives contains elements of death, loss, brokenness, and a longing for peace. Its power, in fact, reflects a longing that is rooted in the truthful themes of the Christian faith. Christians, because of their proximity to the truth, through faith, ought to be able to produce clear reflections on that truth through narrative.

A further strategy to avoiding irrelevance is that of avoiding over-labeling of one's work. When I was a child, I loved to watch the campy old Adam West *Batman* series. In the Bat Cave, every piece of equipment was labeled with a placard, even items that were obvious in their identity. It was laughable to see the over-labeling; the same temptation faces many aspiring writers.

I hope to challenge aspiring writers to create powerful work that is true to the faith by its very foundational elements but is not overtly labeled as "Christian." I hope that they will submit their works to "secular" presses and literary journals, learning to network and pursuing opportunities that will allow them to place their works in mainstream outlets. This is hard work, indeed, as sometimes the Christian publishing world offers easier opportunities for fellow believers, but there is a space that is available for writers who have a missionary's zeal about their narratives. I believe that there are fields that are "white unto harvest" in this marketplace. The secret, though, is to employ this strategy and not be fooled into seeking to please others rather than God. The worst error of judgment a young writer can make is that of compromising in order to seek the applause of the mainstream. Seeking to be true to one's faith commitments while producing culturally engaging works is difficult business, but the works of authors like Flannery O'Connor, John Updike, Marianne Robinson, and many others are proof that this is possible.

Works that engage the culture are ones that follow the Restoration Narrative's insights into the human condition. They are not afraid to depict the imbalance that each of us feels in our lives, and to wrestle with the overwhelming urge we feel to restore that lost equilibrium. This means that Christian writers should be masters of the art of writing about conflict.

The goal of the Christian writer should be a baptized version of Edmundson's injunction: narrative should allow the transformation of lives. It should depict a fallen world that has hope, that finds a way to enable to live the truths of narrative through the power of God.

Earlier I mentioned the story of "Bill," whose journey to conversion began in his readings of literary narrative, particularly Milton's *Paradise Lost*. I find that story all the more poignant because of Milton's Sonnet 19, where the poet pours out his frustrations over the onset of his blindness, which he believed would prevent his writing gifts from being used to their fullest purpose. A few years after he wrote that sonnet, he began the process of writing *Paradise Lost*, which he hoped would "justify the ways of God to men."[5] He hoped, then, that his readers would find a fresh glimpse of God's glory and the power of the gospel.

I can only imagine the joy that Milton would have felt from knowing that his narrative was used in leading a young man to find

---

[5] J. Milton, *Paradise Lost,* in *The Complete Poetry of John Milton,* rev. ed., ed. J. T. Shawcross (New York: Anchor, 1973), book I, line 25; spelling regularized.

salvation. I can further imagine the ecstasy that he would have felt from knowing that in countries that have been closed to biblical witness, missionaries have used *Paradise Lost* as a way to bypass such regulations. In China and many other lands, there are believers whose first glimpse of the gospel came in the pages of an epic poem that was written in the seventeenth century. The Restoration Narrative is powerful indeed. It echoes throughout the world. It changes hearts and souls. It changes eternity.

Epilogue

While researching this book, I took my family to see the movie *Enchanted*. It is about a cartoon princess, Giselle, who is engaged to marry Prince Edward in the magical realm of Andalasia, which is a standard-looking cartoon land, complete with lots of singing and friendly animals. The prince's wicked stepmother opposes the match and tries to prevent it by creating a spell that sends Giselle to the "real world," where Giselle is completely out of sorts. New experiences confront her everywhere she turns, completely altering her view of the world and ushering her into an entire range of experiences that hinder her quest to rejoin her hero, the prince who can give her "true love's kiss." Complications occur, of course, chiefly with her relationship with Robert Phillip, a lawyer. The movie builds toward Giselle's final realization: Robert is her true love, not Edward. This surprises the main characters, of course, but each finds a match in the end, with love surfacing in the new relationships and the evil queen being cast into a kind of Hades as a punishment for her evil actions. The closing screen image is that of Giselle, Robert, and his daughter Morgan, all playing in their apartment, apparently living happily ever after.

I was struck by how closely the plot of the story mirrors that of so many fairy tales, as do most of such fairy tales, so much so that they are spoofs simply by virtue of participating in the genre itself. They all seem to follow the same script. The conflict in all of them derives from evil, which seeks to destroy happiness. In the end, the happiness is restored eternally—at least in the text itself.

That script, of course, is the Restoration Narrative: balance is lost, and we long to have it restored as the story resolves itself. In these stories, true love is the ultimate agent of restoration.

The idea behind "happily ever after" may bring comfort to a children's fairy tale, read at bedtime when young minds crave peace and satisfaction, but every adult knows that life is not geared toward happily ever after. Spouses die of heart attacks and cancers. Children succumb to debilitating diseases. Tornadoes and hurricanes devastate houses and school buildings.

Most of us have had some sort of experience that we look back upon wistfully. When times are hard, we find a kind of succor in those memories that helps us get through. We think back on childhood days of kick and catch in the side yard under a cool blue sky that holds a daytime full moon. We remember the stories that our grandparents have told us. When we gather together with old friends, we tell stories about those times. Ironically, sometimes those good old days were actually hard times that taught us lessons that have endured throughout our lives.

Something in us longs to recapture the feeling of peace and satisfaction that we felt in those old days, in our own personal Edens. We feel the loss of balance that our lives have endured, and we crave a resolution that will restore that balance.

When I was in graduate school in literature, I had several professors who were devotees of Freudian psychology. Freudian approaches to literature emphasize sexual interpretations and symbolism, including explorations of the Id, the Ego, and the Super-Ego. Every time one of these professors worked through a text, I used to chuckle at how often sexually charged symbols came up. I often wondered how much of the sexual obsession was in the text and how much of it was in the professor's own mind. Sometimes the difference was hard to tell.

I do not remember how the topic came up, but one day in a discussion of Faulkner's *The Sound and the Fury*, someone asked our professor about the preponderance of these symbols throughout the text. The professor reminded us of Faulkner's fascination with Freud's writings but also made an interesting statement: "Once Freud has taken over your criticism, he's a hard set of lenses to put away. It's like you can't read anything without seeing him under, over, and behind every rock, bush, and tree, bucket, dome, and tower." To some extent, that's a description of a worldview: it's the lens through which we interpret everything.

A few years ago, I began to hold up the creation–fall–redemption grid to the world around me, wondering how such a fresh view of the world might enhance how I saw everything. First, I began to see it in my discipline, in the way that I viewed the author, the reader, and the text itself. Then I began to see it everywhere I looked: in films, television shows, and song lyrics. Then I started finding it in what seemed like every nook and cranny of the entire created world. By that time, I had a completely different understanding of the declaration in Rom 2:15–16 that God's "law is written on their hearts." Indeed, I saw the Restoration Narrative written on hearts and into stories everywhere I looked.

The night we saw "Enchanted," when we got home, I commented to my wife that even that movie followed the contours of the Restoration Narrative. After pointing out the different parts to her, Lisa just smiled at me and said, "You know, it shouldn't be that surprising to you by this point. After all, God's story is the only Story we really ever know."

Indeed, the Master Author's grand tale, the tale of His great love, our great need, and His great restoration and glorious redemptive work is the only story that we know. Its echoes resound everywhere.

Sources

Alter, Robert. *The Art of Biblical Narrative.* New York: Basic Books, 1983.

Aristotle. "On the Art of Poetry." In *Classical Literary Criticism*, trans. T. S. Dorsch, pp. 29–76. New York: Penguin, 1965.

Augustine. *Confessions.* Translated by F. J. Sheed. Lanham, MD: Sheed and Ward, 1944.

Axelrod, Rise B., and Charles R. Cooper. *The St. Martin's Guide to Writing.* 6th ed. Boston: Bedford / St. Martin's, 2001.

Bede. *Ecclesiastical History of the English People.* Translated by Leo Sherley-Price. Rev. ed. New York: Penguin, 1968.

Beowulf: A New Verse Translation (bilingual edition). Translated by Seamus Heaney. New York: W. W. Norton, 2001.

Bertrand, Mark. *(Re)Thinking Worldview: Learning to Think, Live, and Speak in This World.* Wheaton, IL: Crossway, 2007.

Brown, Dan. *The Da Vinci Code.* New York: Doubleday, 2003.

Brown, James S., and Scott D. Yarbrough. *A Practical Introduction to Literary Study.* Upper Saddle River, NJ: Pearson Prentice Hall, 2005.

Brown, Raymond E. *The Community of the Beloved Disciple.* New York: Paulist, 1979.

Budziszewski, J. *Written on the Heart: The Case for Natural Law.* Downers Grove: IVP, 1997.

Camus, Albert. *The Stranger.* Translated by Stuart Gilbert. New York: Vintage, 1946.

Capra, Fritjof. *The Tao of Physics: An Exploration of the Parallels be-tween Modern Physics and Eastern Mysticism.* 4th ed. Boston: Shambhala, 2000.

Catechism of the Catholic Church. New York: Image / Doubleday, 1994.

Cervantes, Miguel. *Don Quixote.* In *The Norton Anthology of World Lit-erature,* Vol. C: *1500 to 1650,* edited by Sarah Lawall, pp. 2671–2782. Translated by Samuel Putnam. 2nd ed. New York: W. W. Nor-ton, 2002.

Colson, Charles, and Nancy Pearcey. *How Now Shall We Live?* Wheaton, IL: Tyndale House, 1999.

Crane, Stephen. *The Red Badge of Courage and Selected Prose and Po-etry.* 3rd ed., with an introduction by William M. Gibson. New York: Holt, Rinehart, and Winston, 1968.

Criswell, W. A. *Why I Preach that the Bible Is Literally True.* Nashville: Broadman Press, 1969.

Crouch, Andy. *Culture Making: Recovering Our Creative Calling.* Downers Grove: InterVarsity Press, 2008.

DeYoung, Kevin, and Ted Kluck. *Why We're Not Emergent (by Two Guys Who Should Be).* Chicago: Moody, 2008.

Dockery, David S. *Renewing Minds: Serving Church and Society through Christian Higher Education.* Nashville: B&H Academic, 2007.

Dorsch, T. S. "Introduction." In *Classical Literary Criticism.* Pp. 7–28. New York: Penguin, 1965.

Douglass, Frederick. *Narrative of the Life of Frederick Douglass* (1845). New York: Dover, 1995.

Eagleton, Terry. *After Theory.* New York: Basic Books, 2003.

Edmundson, Mark. "Against Readings." *The Chronicle of Higher Educa-tion,* April 24, 2009, http://chronicle.com/weekly/v55/i33/33b00601 .htm.

———. *Why Read?* New York: Bloomsbury, 2004.

Eldredge, John. *Epic: The Story God Is Telling and the Role that Is Yours to Play.* Nashville: Thomas Nelson, 2004.

Eliot, T. S. "Philip Massinger." In *The Sacred Wood: Essays on Poetry and Criticism.* 1922; repr. New York: Dover, 1979.

The Epic of Gilgamesh. In *The Norton Anthology of World Literature,* vol. A: *Beginnings to A.D. 100.* 2nd ed. Translated by N. K. Sandars. Pp. 10–40. New York: W. W. Norton, 2002.

Erickson, Millard J. *Christian Theology.* Grand Rapids: Baker, 1985.

Faulkner, William. "Banquet Speech (December 10, 1950)." In *Nobel Lectures, Literature 1901–1967*, edited by Horst Frenz. Amsterdam: Elsevier Publishing Company, 1969. Posted at http://nobelprize.org/ nobel_prizes/literature/laureates/1949/faulkner-speech.html.

———. *Faulkner in the University: Class Conferences at the University of Virginia 1957–1958*. Edited by Frederick L. Gwynn and Joseph L. Blotner. Charlottesville, VA: University of Virginia Press, 1959.

———. "An Introduction for *The Sound and the Fury*," unpublished 1933 version. *The Southern Review* (1972): 8; pp. 705–710; reproduced at "Faulkner's Introductions to *The Sound and the Fury*" http://www .usask.ca/english/faulkner/main/intros1933/index.html.

———. "A Rose for Emily." *The Heath Introduction to Literature*, 3rd edition. Edited by Alice S. Landy. Lexington, MA: D. C. Heath, 1988. Pp. 198–206.

———. *The Sound and the Fury*. Corrected text edition by Noel Polk. New York: Vintage International, 1990.

Fish, Stanley. *Is There a Text in This Class: The Authority of Interpretive Communities*. Boston: Harvard University Press, 1982.

Fitzgerald, F. Scott. *The Great Gatsby*. New York: Scribners, 1992.

Freytag, Gustav. *An Exposition of Dramatic Composition and Art*. Translated by Elias J. MacEwan as *Freytag's Technique of the Drama*. New York: Benjamin Blom, 1968.

George, Robert P. *Making Men Moral: Civil Liberties and Public Morality*. New York: Oxford University Press, 1995.

Goldberg, Michael. *Theology and Narrative: A Critical Introduction*. Eugene, OR: Wipf and Stock, 2001.

Gonzalez, Guillermo, and Jay W. Richards. *The Privileged Planet: How Our Place in the Cosmos Is Designed for Discovery*. Washington, DC: Regnery, 2004.

Harmon, William, and Hugh Holman. *A Handbook to Literature*. 10th ed. Upper Saddle River, NJ: Pearson Prentice Hall, 2006.

Hauerwas, Stanley. *A Community of Character: Toward a Constructive Christian Social Ethic*. South Bend, IN: University of Notre Dame Press, 1981.

Heulin, Scott. "Peregrination, Hermeneutics, Hospitality: On the Way to a Theologically Informed General Hermeneutics." *Literature and Theology* 22 (2008): 223–36.

Hirsch, E. D., Jr. *Cultural Literacy: What Every American Needs to Know*. New York: Vintage, 1988.

Hopkins, Gerard Manley. "God's Grandeur." In *The Norton Anthology of English Literature: The Major Authors*. Edited by M. H. Abrams, pp. 2127–28. 6th ed. New York: W. W. Norton, 1996.

Ishiguro, Kazuo. *Never Let Me Go*. New York: Vintage, 2006.

Jacobs, Alan. *A Theology of Reading: The Hermeneutics of Love*. Cambridge, MA: Westview, 2001.

Joyce, James. "Araby." In *The Heath Introduction to Literature*, edited by Alice S. Landry, pp. 300–304. 6th ed. Lexington, MA: Heath, 1988.

Keats, John. "Ode on a Grecian Urn." In *The Norton Anthology of English Literature: The Major Authors*, edited by M. H. Abrams, pp. 1793–1795. 6th ed. New York: W. W. Norton, 1996.

Lamott, Anne. *Bird by Bird: Some Instructions on Writing and Life*. New York: Anchor, 1994.

Lewis, C. S. *The Abolition of Man*. New York: HarperSanFrancisco, 1974.

———. *God in the Dock*. Edited by Walter Hooper. Grand Rapids: Eerdmans, 1970.

———. *The Magician's Nephew*. London: Grafton, 1955.

———. *Mere Christianity*. New York: Macmillan, 1952.

———. *Surprised by Joy: The Shape of My Early Life*. Boston: Houghton, Mifflin, Harcourt, 1995.

Lindvall, E. K. *Read-Aloud Bible Stories*. Chicago: Moody, 1986.

Machiavelli. *The Prince and Selected Discourses*. Translated by Daniel Donno. New York: Bantam, 1966.

Markos, Louis. *From Achilles to Christ: Why Christians Should Read the Pagan Classics*. Downers Grove: IVP Academic, 2007.

Marlowe, Christopher. *Doctor Faustus*. New York: Signet, 2001.

Martin, Steve. "Serious Dogs." In *Cruel Shoes*. Pp. 31–36. New York: G. P. Putnam's Sons, 1979.

Mathabane, Mark. *Kaffir Boy: An Autobiography; The True Story of a Black Youth's Coming of Age in Apartheid South Africa*. New York: Free Press, 1998.

McGrath, Alister. "Address to CCCU International Forum." CCCU International Forum, Grapevine TX, April 1, 2006.

McQuade, Donald, Robert Atwan, Martha Banta, Justin Kaplan, David Minter, Cecelia Tichi, and Helen Vendler, eds. *The Harper American Literature*. Compact edition. Philadelphia: Harper and Row, 1987.

McQuade, Donald, Robert Atwan, Martha Banta, Justin Kaplan, David Minter, Robert Stepto, Cecelia Tichi, and Helen Vendler, eds. *The*

Harper American Literature. Compact 2nd edition. Philadelphia: Harper and Row, 1996.

Meeter, Glenn. "Bible." In *A William Faulkner Encyclopedia*. Edited by Robert W. Hamblin and Charles A. Peek, pp. 40–42. Santa Barbara, CA: Greenwood, 1999.

Middleton, Darren J. N. *Theology after Reading: Christian Imagination and the Power of Fiction*. Waco: Baylor University Press, 2008.

Miller, David G. *The Word Made Flesh Made Word: The Failure and Redemption of Metaphor in Edward Taylor's* Christographia. Selinsgrove, PA: Susquehanna University Press, 1995.

Miller, Donald. *Blue Like Jazz: Nonreligious Thoughts on Christian Spirituality*. Nashville: Thomas Nelson, 2003.

Milton, John. "Sonnet 19." In *The Complete Poetry of John Milton*. Edited by John T. Shawcross, pp. 242–43. Rev. ed. New York: Anchor, 1973.

———. *Paradise Lost*. In *The Complete Poetry of John Milton*. Edited by John T. Shawcross. Rev. ed. pp. 249–518. New York: Anchor, 1973.

Moliere. *Tartuffe*. Translated by Prudence L. Steiner. Indianapolis: Hackett, 2008.

North, John. "The Text's the Thing: Reflections from the Humanities." In *The Two Tasks of the Christian Scholar: Redeeming the Soul, Redeeming the Mind*. Edited by William Lane Craig and Paul M. Gould, pp. 155–76. Wheaton, IL: Crossway, 2007.

O'Connor, Flannery. "A Good Man Is Hard to Find." In *The Heath Introduction to Literature,* edited by Alice S. Landry, pp. 397–410. 6th ed. Lexington, MA: Heath, 1988.

"One in Four Americans Read No Books Last Year," Manchester *Guardian*, August 22, 2007, posted at (http://www.guardian.co.uk /books/2007/aug/22/news.

Osborne, Grant R. *The Hermeneutical Spiral: A Comprehensive Introduction to Biblical Interpretation*. Rev. ed. Downers Grove: IVP Academic, 2006.

Owen, Stephen, trans. "Chung-Tzu, Please." In *The Norton Anthology of World Literature,* Vol. A: *Beginnings to A.D. 100,* edited by Jerome W. Clinton et al., pp. 817. 2nd ed. New York: W. W. Norton, 2002.

Paglia, Camille. "Religion and the Arts in America." *Arion: A Journal of Humanities and the Classics* 15 (Spring / Summer 2007): 1. http://www.bu.edu/arion/Paglia.htm.

Pinsky, Robert. *The Life of David*. New York, Shocken, 2005.

Richardson, Don. *Eternity in Their Hearts: Startling Evidence of Belief in the One True God in Hundreds of Cultures throughout the World.* Ventura, CA: Regal, 2006.

Ricouer, Paul. *Freud and Philosophy: An Essay on Interpretation.* New Haven: Yale University Press, 1970.

Ryken, Leland, and Philip Graham Ryken. *ESV Literary Study Bible.* Wheaton, IL: Crossway, 2007.

Sandars, N. K., trans. *The Epic of Gilgamesh.* In *The Norton Anthology of World Literature*, vol. A: *Beginnings to A.D. 100,* edited by Jerome W. Clinton et al., pp. 10–40. 2nd ed. New York: W. W. Norton, 2002.

Schaeffer, Francis. A. *How Should We Then Live? The Rise and Decline of Western Thought and Culture.* 50th anniversary ed. Wheaton, IL: Crossway, 2005.

Shakespeare, William. *The Tragedy of Hamlet, Prince of Denmark.* In *The Riverside Shakespeare.* Pp. 1135–97. Dallas: Houghton Mifflin, 1974.

———. *The Tragedy of Macbeth.* In *The Riverside Shakespeare.* Pp. 1306–42. Dallas: Houghton Mifflin, 1974.

———. *Measure for Measure.* In *The Riverside Shakespeare.* Pp. 545–86. Dallas: Houghton Mifflin, 1974.

———. "Sonnets." In *The Riverside Shakespeare,* Pp. 1745–80. Dallas: Houghton Mifflin, 1974.

Sire, James W. *Naming the Elephant: Worldview as a Concept.* Downers Grove: IVP, 2004.

Smith, James K. A. *Who's Afraid of Postmodernism: Taking Derrida, Lyotard, and Foucault to Church.* Grand Rapids: Baker, 2006.

Sophocles. *Oedipus the King (Oedipus Rex).* In *The Norton Anthology of World Literature,* vol. A: *Beginnings to A.D. 100.* Edited by Jerome W. Clinton et al., pp. 617–47. Translated by Robert Fagles. 2nd ed. New York: W. W. Norton, 2002.

Spenser, Edmund. "A Letter of the Authors [to Walter Raleigh]." In *The Faerie Queen,* ed. A. C. Hamilton. New York: Longman, 1977.

Stowe, Harriet Beecher. *Uncle Tom's Cabin.* 1852; repr., New York: Barnes & Noble, 2003.

ten Boom, Corrie. *The Hiding Place.* New York: Bantam, 1971.

Thigpen, Paul. "Interviewed by Darren J. N. Middleton." *Theology after Reading: Christian Imagination and the Power of Fiction.* Waco: Baylor University Press, 2008.

Thoreau, Henry David. *Walden.* 1854; repr., New York: Dover, 2001.

Tillyard, E. M. W. *The Elizabethan World Picture.* New York: Vintage, 1959.

Tolkien, J. R. R. "*Beowulf:* The Monsters and the Critics." In *Interpretations of "Beowulf": a Critical Anthology.* Edited by R. D. Fulk, pp. 14–44. Bloomington: Indiana University Press, 1991.

Twain, Mark (Samuel L. Clemens). *Adventures of Huckleberry Finn.* Centennial facsimile edition. New York: Harper & Row, 1987.

Vanhoozer, Kevin J. *Is There a Meaning in This Text?: The Bible, the Reader, and the Morality of Literary Knowledge.* Grand Rapids: Zondervan, 1998.

Venkatesananda, Swami, trans. *The Rāmāyana of Valmiki.* In *The Norton Anthology of World Literature*, vol A: *Beginnings to A.D. 100,* edited by Jerome W. Clinton et al., pp. 890–952. 2nd ed. New York: W. W. Norton, 2002.

Virgil. *The Aeneid.* In *The Norton Anthology of World Literature*, Vol A: *Beginnings to A.D. 100.* Edited by Jerome W. Clinton et al. Translated by Robert Fitzgerald. 2nd ed. Pp. 1052–1133. New York: W. W. Norton, 2002.

Washington, Booker. T. *Up from Slavery.* New York: Dover, 1995.

Welty, Eudora. *On Writing*, with an introduction by Richard Bausch. New York: Modern Library, 2002.

Wicker, Benjamin, and Jonathan Witt. *A Meaningful World: How the Arts and Sciences Reveal the Genius of Nature.* Downers Grove: IVP Academic, 2006.

Wordsworth, William. "Sonnet XXXIII: The World Is Too Much with Us" (1807). In *The Works of William Wordsworth,* p. 259. Hertfordshire: Wordsworth Editions / Cumberland House, 1994.

Young, William P. *The Shack.* Los Angeles: Windblown Media, 2007.

Yeats, William Butler. "The Second Coming." In *The Norton Anthology of English Literature*: *The Major Authors*, edited by M. H. Abrams, p. 2280. 6th ed. New York: W. W. Norton, 1996.

Zappa, Frank, and Peter Occhiogrosso. *The Real Frank Zappa Book.* New York: Touchstone, 1989. http://en.wikiquote.org/wiki/Frank_Zappa.

Zukav, Gary. *The Dancing Wu Li Masters: An Overview of the New Physics.* New York: HarperOne, 2001.

About the Author

Gene C. Fant Jr. is Professor of English at Union University in Jackson, Tennessee. He holds degrees from James Madison University (B.S. in anthropology), Old Dominion University (M.A. in English), the New Orleans Baptist Theological Seminary (M.Div. in biblical languages), and the University of Southern Mississippi (Ph.D. in Renaissance English litcrature and a post-doctoral M.Ed. in educational leadership). He has won awards in poetry, fiction writing, songwriting, and nonfiction, including the Daub-Maher Prize from the Southeastern Conference on Christianity and Literature and two Amy Foundation Writing Awards for his newspaper editorials. In addition to memberships in the Conference on Christianity and Literature and the Modern Language Association, Dr. Fant serves on the steering committee of the Literature of the Bible study group of the Evangelical Theological Society. In 2005, he received the Newell Innovative Teaching Award at Union University, where he also serves as the dean of the College of Arts and Sciences. Married to Lisa, he is the father of twins, Ethan and Emily.

Name Index

Aeschylus *9*
Alter, R. *60, 185*
Aristotle *75, 89–92, 94, 96–97, 115, 185*
Augustine *18, 21, 25, 123–24, 135, 147–48, 167, 185*
Axelrod, R. B. *5, 185*

Barfield, O. *26*
Bede *82–84, 185*
Bertrand, M. *31, 140, 152, 185*
Brown, D. *11–12, 49, 185*
Brown, J. S. *7, 93, 185*
Brown, R. E. *139, 185*
Budziszewski, J. *59, 185*
Bunyan, J. *169*

Camus, A. *53, 151–52, 185*
Capra, F. *81, 186*
Cervantes, M. *9, 118, 186*
Colson, C. *xvi, 64, 130–31, 186*
Cooper, C. R. *5, 185*
Crane, S. *26–27, 186*
Criswell, W. A. *37, 67, 186*
Crouch, A. *186*

Dante *9, 18, 21, 25*
DeYoung, K. *3–4, 58, 186*
Dickinson, E. *9*
Dockery, D. *ix, 65, 186*
Dorsch, T. S. *89–90 185–86*
Douglass, F. *11, 53, 186*

Eagleton, T. *27–28, 32, 186*

Edmundson, M. *28, 149, 176, 178, 186*
Eldredge, J. *100, 186*
Eliot, T. S. *18, 25, 143–44, 146–47, 167, 186*
Erickson, M. J. *57–58, 67, 186*

Faulkner, W. *21, 36, 53, 55, 139, 182–83, 187*
Fish, S. *18, 32, 54, 187*
Fitzgerald, F. S. *64, 121, 163, 187*
Freytag, G. *92–94, 96–97, 187*

George, R. P. *59, 187*
Goethe *9*
Goldberg, M. *60, 187*
Gonzalez, G. *73, 187*

Handel, G. *19*
Harmon, W. *25, 91, 93–94, 187*
Hauerwas, S. *60, 187*
Heulin, S. *32, 187*
Hirsch, E. D., Jr. *20, 148, 187*
Holman, H. *25, 91, 93–94, 187*
Homer *9*
Hopkins, G. M. *146, 159, 188*
Huxley, A. *113*

Ishiguro, K. *xv, 14, 188*

Jacobs, A. *31–32, 175, 188*
Joyce, J. *95, 117, 188*

Kafka, F. *113*

Keats, J.   *xiii–xiv, 122, 188*
Kluck, T.   *3–4, 58, 186*

Lamott, A.   *49, 188*
Lewis, C. S.   *18, 26, 59, 72–73,
   81–82, 105–6, 126, 143, 145,
   148, 162, 167, 171, 188*
Lindvall, E. K.   *138, 188*
Longfellow, H. W.   *24–25, 143*
Lyotard, J.   *104*

Machiavelli   *39, 188*
Markos, L.   *106, 188*
Marlowe, C.   *124, 188*
Martin, S.   *8, 188*
Mathabane, M.   *53, 188*
Maugham, S.   *119*
McGrath, A.   *104, 188*
McQuade, D.   *24–25, 188*
Meeter, G.   *139–40, 189*
Middleton, D. J. N.   *19, 153, 189*
Miller, D.   *96, 98–100, 141–42,
   189*
Miller, D. G.   *40, 189*
Milton, J.   *19, 63, 114, 127, 130,
   133, 144, 167, 171, 178, 189*
Moliere   *53, 189*

North, J.   *27, 140, 144, 147, 189*

Obsorne, G. R.   *18*
Occhiogrosso, P.   *77, 191*
O'Connor, F.   *109, 125, 174,
   178, 189*
Oedipus   *116*
Orwell, G.   *xv, 113*
Osborne, G. R.   *189*
Ovid   *114, 122*
Owen, S.   *189*

Paglia, C.   *19, 20, 189*
Pearcey, N.   *xvi, 64, 130–31, 186*

Perrine, L.   *xiv*
Pinsky, R.   *20, 189*
Plato   *89*

Richards, J. W.   *73, 187*
Richardson, D.   *106, 190*
Ricouer, P.   *26, 190*
Ryken, L.   *39–40, 190*
Ryken, P. G.   *39–40, 190*

Sandars, N. K.   *120, 186, 190*
Schaeffer, F. A.   *130, 190*
Shakespeare, W.   *5, 9, 13, 20, 22,
   25, 53, 122, 144, 152, 167, 190*
Sire, J.   *9*
Sire, J. W.   *9, 74, 190*
Smith, J. K. A.   *31, 190*
Socrates   *89*
Sophocles   *14, 91–92, 115–16,
   190*
Spenser, E.   *25, 154, 190*
Stowe, H. B.   *11, 190*

Taylor, E.   *40*
ten Boom, C.   *155, 190*
Thigpen, P.   *30–33, 190*
Thoreau, H. D.   *151, 191*
Tillyard, E. M. W.   *29, 191*
Tolkien, J. R. R.   *9, 18, 105,
   140–41, 167, 191*
Twain, M.   *1, 6, 144, 191*

Valmiki, M.   *191*
Vanhoozer, K. J.   *18, 191*
Venkatesananda, S.   *112, 191*
Virgil   *152–53, 191*

Washington, B. T.   *35, 49, 191*
Welty, E.   *28, 152, 191*
Wicker, B.   *4, 191*
Witt, J.   *4, 191*
Woolf, V.   *9*

Wordsworth, W. *xiii, 143, 191*

Yarbrough, S. D. *7, 93, 185*
Yeats, W. B. *111, 191*

Young, W. P. *12, 60, 169–70, 191*

Zappa, F. *77, 191*
Zukav, G. *81, 191*

Subject Index

A

Aeneid, The *14, 22, 122, 147, 149, 152–53*
allegory *21–26, 99*
Aristotelian Poetics *89–92, 96, 149*
authorship *44–47, 49–50, 52–54, 56, 61, 67*

B

Biblical influences on literature *20–21, 140*
Bidungsroman/Journey of Experience *94–96*

C

Christian intellectual tradition *12, 19–20, 22, 25, 31–33, 142–147, 162, 167, 170, 178, 183*
Christian worldview *62, 64–70, 74, 131*
  creation/balance *66, 69–70, 72–75, 81–82, 97, 99, 101–103, 107, 111–114, 117, 166, 182*
  fall/imbalance *66, 69–70, 72, 74, 82–84, 96–97, 99, 101–103, 107, 113–115, 117–119, 123, 125–126, 166, 169, 174, 176, 182*
  mission *31, 64, 131–132, 164*
  redemption/restoration *21, 66, 70, 72–74, 82–83, 96–97, 99, 101–103, 107, 117–120, 119–121, 123, 125–126, 166, 169, 171, 174, 182*

E

epiphany *95–97, 99, 117–118*

F

Freytag's triangle or pyramid *92–94, 96–97, 99*

G

general revelation   *46, 54, 56–61, 70, 72–73, 81–82, 85, 100–101, 106, 124*
God as Author-Creator   *40, 42, 44–48, 50–51, 54, 56, 61–62, 66–67, 71–72, 86, 100–101, 104, 174, 183*

H

hermeneutics   *2, 5–6, 15, 17–20, 25, 28, 33–34, 39, 62, 86, 101, 149, 175*
   "hermeneutics of optimism"   *26, 28–29, 31–33*
   "hermeneutics of suspicion"   *26–27, 31*

L

literary criticism   *5, 15, 18–19, 22–28, 32, 37, 53–54, 64, 86, 89, 104, 149, 160*

M

Macbeth   *20, 22, 53*
meta-narrative   *103–105, 166*
metaphor   *37–44, 47, 61–62, 80, 100, 104*

N

narrative   *4–20, 21, 24–25, 28–33, 37–38, 45, 48–49, 53–54, 59, 66, 89–90, 92, 94, 96–100, 106–108, 113, 118, 122, 124, 127, 132–133, 136, 139–142, 145–154, 156–158, 161, 171–173, 175–176, 178–180*
narrative theology   *59–60, 100*
natural law   *58–59, 87*

P

Paradise Lost   *19, 114, 127, 133, 171, 178–180*

R

reading reflectively   *148–149*
reading relationally   *149–152, 149–153*
religious pluralism   *3–4, 58*
Restoration Narrative   *86, 97, 99–101, 103, 107, 124, 133, 137, 142–143, 158, 165, 167, 171–172, 175–176, 179, 182–184*
   in biblical narratives   *101–103, 166*
   in *The Gilgamesh Epic*   *117, 119–121*
   in *Oedipus Rex*   *113, 115–116*
   in *The Rāmāyana*   *111–113, 157, 165–166*
Restoration Principle   *69–70, 72–74, 76, 78–79, 82, 85, 96*
   defined   *70–71*
   in art   *77*
   in biology   *76, 78–80*
   in geology   *75*
   in hydrology   *76*
   in literature   *86*
   in music   *76*
   in physics   *74–75*

S

Sound and the Fury, The   *53, 55, 182*
special revelation   *54, 57–61, 66–68, 72, 84, 100–101*

T

Tao, The   *59, 81–82*

Scripture Index

Genesis

6:2 *101*
6–9 *101*
18:25 *43*
22 *102, 166*
22:6 *159, 167*

Exodus

15:3 *43*
31:18 *44–45*

Leviticus

19:18 *54*

Deuteronomy

4:9 *xi*
6:4 *54*

Judges

4 *138*
9:7–15 *16*

1 Samuel

9:2 *21*
16–17 *20*

2 Samuel

12 *16*
19:4 *21*

Job

19:25 *41*

Psalms

19 *72*
19:1 *60*
19:1–4 *63, 70*
19:14 *41*
23 *41, 80*
23:3 *109*
25:5 *50*
25:10 *50*
26:3 *50*
40:10–11 *50*
42:1–2 *79*
43:3 *50*
50:6 *71*
51:12 *119*
57:3 *50*
61:7 *50*
63:1 *80*
85:10 *50*
85:11 *50*
89:2 *71*
89:5 *71*
89:14 *50*
89:26 *59*
97:6 *71, 85*
107:9 *80*
115:1 *50*

Proverbs

1:1–6 *17*
1:7 *18*
25:21 *80*

Ecclesiastes

1:18   *95*

Isaiah

41:14   *41*
64:8   *43*

Jeremiah

18:1–12   *16*

Ezekiel

15   *16*
16   *16*
17   *16*
17:1–2   *21*
24   *16*

Daniel

1:17   *135, 148*
1:20   *135*
5   *44*

Matthew

4   *22*
7:24–26   *59*
13   *16*
13:34–35   *16*
13:36   *16*
15:10–12   *153*
22:40   *54*
25:21   *176*
25:31–46   *80*
28:19–20   *132*

Mark

10   *103*
12:30   *132*

Luke

4:17   *44*

24:27   *16*
24:32   *16*

John

1:17   *51*
3:16   *166*
4   *80, 103*
4:7   *80*
4:13–14   *80*
6:35   *41*
8:6   *35, 44*
8:12   *41*
10:7   *41*
10:9   *40*
10:11   *41*
14:6   *41, 51*
15:1   *41*
17:24   *56*
18:38   *105*

Acts

2   *173*
5   *103*
8:26–40   *17*
8:30   *17*
8:30–31   *1*
8:31   *17*
11   *153*
17   *156*

Romans

1:16–20   *71*
1:18–20   *46*
1:18–25   *51*
1:20   *72*
2:14–16   *72*
2:15   *45, 87*
2:15–16   *183*
5:8   *56*
5:12   *177*
8:29   *48*

12:1–8   *13*
12:2   *132*
15:4   *153*

1 Corinthians

2:14–15   *4*
2:16   *132*
3:1–3   *156*
12:12   *13*
13:11   *141*
15:51–53   *123*

2 Corinthians

10:3–4   *132*

Galatians

4:24   *21*

Ephesians

1:4   *56*
2:10   *44*
4:11   *61*

Philippians

4:8   *154–55*

Colossians

1:19–20   *129, 131*
1:20   *101, 123*

2 Timothy

2:22   *119*
3:16–17   *154*

Hebrews

11   *103*
11:10   *43*
11:32   *103*
12:2   *xv, 45*

James

1:22   *149*
1:27   *177*
2:26   *133*

1 John

3:23   *176*
4:16   *42*
4:19   *56*

Revelation

13:8   *56*
21:4   *82*